CONTENTS

CONTENTS CONTINUED

Introduction

Progressive Jazz Lead Guitar Method takes an innovative approach to learning Jazz improvisation on guitar. *While most books on improvisation assume the student is already quite an accomplished guitarist, this one requires only a rudimentary knowledge of playing in the open and first positions. Beginning with the C major scale in the open position, the student is quickly introduced to Jazz sounds and phrases, along with a simple method for playing over any major key chord progression.*

As well as knowing what notes to play, the other essential element in Jazz improvisation is mastery of rhythm, particularly swing rhythms. In many methods, this is already assumed, or not touched on until much later in the learning process, but in this book, it is introduced very early on, and continued throughout the book.

The later sections of the book deal with a system of fingerings which cover the whole fretboard, and a demonstration of the use of chord arpeggios and modes both within keys and modulating. Chromatic and Blues notes are also introduced, although these will be dealt with in detail in the follow up book - Progressive Jazz Lead Guitar Technique.

To ensure you develop a good time feel right from the start, it is recommended that you use a metromome or drum machine when practicing all the examples in the book. It would also be helpful to play along with the recording that accompanies the book. If you are serious about music, a good teacher can often help you progress much quicker than you can on your own.

Keep practicing, keep playing and have fun,

Peter Gelling.

Progressive

JAZZ
LEAD GUITAR

METHOD

By

Peter Gelling

Acknowledgments
Cover Photograph: Phil
Martin
Photographs: Phil Martin

Instruments supplied by
Derringers Music

LTP Publications Pty. Ltd.
Email:
info@learntoplaymusic.com
or visit our website at:
www.learntoplaymusic.com

I.S.B.N. 1 864691 74 3
Order Code:
   CD Pack   CP-69174

Using the Compact Disc

The accompanying compact disc includes all the examples in this book. The book shows you where to put your fingers and what technique to use and the recording lets you hear how each example should sound. Practice the examples slowly at first, gradually increasing tempo. Once you are confident you can play the example evenly without stopping the beat, try playing along with the recording. You will hear a drum beat at the beginning of each example, to lead you into the example and to help you keep time. To play along with the CD your guitar must be in tune with it. If you have tuned using an electronic tuner (see below) your guitar will already be in tune with the CD. A small diagram of a compact disc with a number as shown below indicates a recorded example. Many of the tracks on the CD contain more than one example. In these cases, index points are used (1.0, 1.1, 1.2 etc). If your CD player has an index points function, you can select each example individually. If not, each example will automatically follow the previous one. The first track on the CD contains the notes of the six open strings of the guitar. 1.0 is the 6th string (low E)1.1 is the open A string, 1.3 is the open D string, etc.

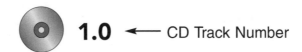 **1.0** ← CD Track Number

Tuning Your Guitar

Before you commence each lesson or practice session you will need to tune your guitar. If your guitar is out of tune everything you play will sound incorrect even though you are holding the correct notes. The easiest and most accurate way to tune your guitar is by using an **electronic tuner.** An electronic tuner allows you to tune each string individually to the tuner, by indicating whether the notes are sharp (too high), or flat (too low). If you have an electric

Electronic Tuner

guitar you can plug it directly in to the tuner. If you have an acoustic guitar the tuner will have an inbuilt microphone. There are several types of electronic guitar tuners but most are relatively inexpensive and simple to operate. Tuning using other methods is difficult for beginning guitarists and it takes many months to master. So we recommend you purchase an electronic tuner, particularly if you do not have a guitar teacher or a friend who can tune it for you. Also if your guitar is way out of tune you can always take it to your local music store so they can tune it for you. Once a guitar has been tuned correctly it should only need minor adjustments before each practice session. For a complete description of how to tune your guitar, see *Progressive How to Tune the Guitar.*

Fretboard Diagrams

Fretboard diagrams are given throughout this book to show which patterns and fingerings are given for each scale. To know how to read the diagrams, study the following illustration.

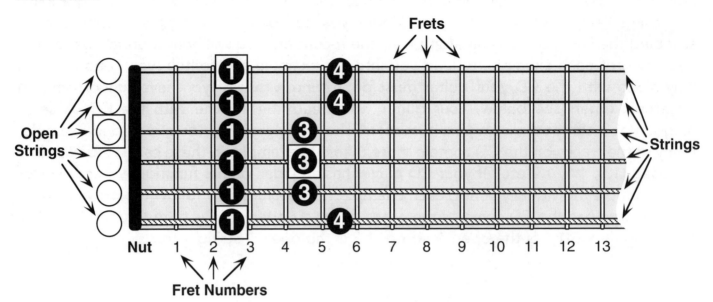

● or ○ = A note used in the scale or pattern.

■ or □ = Indicates the note is the key note of the scale.

❷ = The number refers to the left hand fingering.

Left Hand Fingering

❶ Index Finger
❷ Middle Finger
❸ Ring Finger
❹ Little Finger

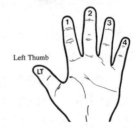

Tablature

This book uses standard music notation and tablature notation. If you cannot read music notes, use the tab written below the music. Music readers will need to look at the tab to see what technique is being used to play certain notes (e.g. hammer-on, slide etc).

Tablature is a method of indicating the position of notes on the fretboard. There are six "tab" lines each representing one of the six strings on the guitar.

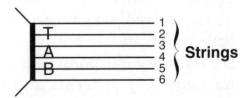

When a number is placed on one of the lines, it indicates the fret location of the note e.g.

This indicates the **seventh** fret of the **5th** string (an **E** note).

This indicates the **3rd** string open (a **G** note).

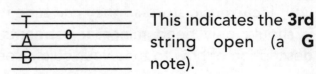

Technique

Right Hand Position

There are basically two right hand positions when using the pick. The first is closing the fingers of the right hand, and the second position is opening the hand across the face of the guitar. Try both positions and decide which one you are most comfortable with.

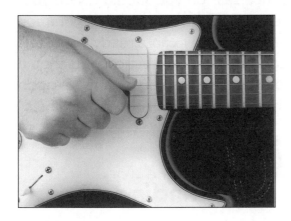

Left Hand Technique

All notes must be fretted with the tips of the fingers and positioned as close as practical to the fretwires.

Fingertips as close as practical to fretwires.

Left Hand Position

There are basically two positions for the left hand. In most cases the left hand thumb should be positioned behind the neck of the guitar with the fingers evenly arched over the fretboard. When using techniques such as the bend, release bend, vibrato etc. you may find it more comfortable to have the left hand thumb in a higher position, wrapped over the top of the fretboard.

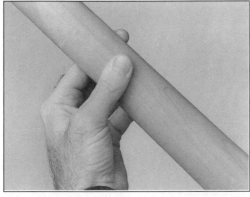

Thumb positioned behind neck.

Thumb positioned over the neck.

Approach to Practice

It is important to have a correct approach to practice. Get one small piece of information and learn it well before going on to the next topic. Make sure each new thing you learn is thoroughly worked into your playing. This way you won't forget it, and you can build on everything you learn. You will benefit more from several short practices (e.g. 30 minutes per day) than one or two long sessions per week. This is especially so in the early stages, because of the basic nature of the material being studied. In a practice session you should divide your time evenly between the study of new material and the revision of past work. It is a common mistake for semi-advanced students to practice only the pieces they can already play well. Although this is more enjoyable, it is not a very satisfactory method of practice. You should also try to correct mistakes and experiment with new ideas. To be sure you develop a good sense of time, it is **essential** that you always practice with a metronome or drum machine.

Practice Position

Sitting

1. Sit up straight on the front part of the chair as shown in the photo below.

2. Raise your right leg by crossing it over your left leg or by placing your right foot on a footstool (as shown in the photo below). Then place your guitar on your right leg.

3. The guitar should be close to your body in an upright position with the neck pointing slightly upwards.

The main aim is to be comfortable and have easy access to the guitar fretboard. A music stand will also be helpful.

Standing

Use a wide guitar strap and adjust it to a comfortable length.

SECTION 1
Basic Jazz Sounds and Techniques

LESSON ONE

THE MAJOR SCALE

To begin playing Jazz lead guitar, you will need to be familiar with the major scale. A major scale is a pattern of eight notes in alphabetical order that produce the familiar sound:

Do Re Mi Fa So La Ti Do

The **C major scale** contains these notes in the following order:

C D E F G A B C

The distance between each note is two frets except for **EF** and **BC** where the distance is only one fret.

The distance of two frets is called a **tone** indicated by **T**.

The distance of one fret is called a **semitone** indicated by **ST**.

The major scale is probably the most common scale used in music. Written below is one octave of the C major scale in the open position. Make sure you know it from memory.

 2

Below is a diagram of all of the natural notes in the open position. They are all notes of the C major scale, even though the lowest note of the pattern is E and the highest note is G. The key note **C** is indicated twice. This pattern can be described as the full open position fingering of the C major scale.

C Major Scale in Open Position

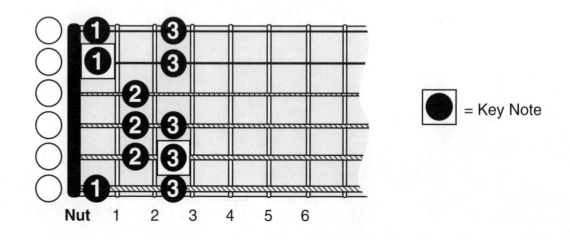

Here are the notes from the diagram written in standard music notation and tablature.

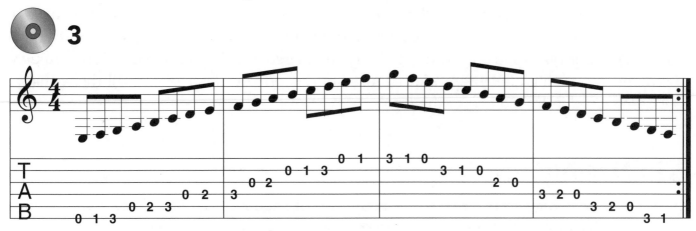

These notes can be used to play literally thousands of melodies in the key of C major. It is not necessary to always start and finish on the note C. Depending on which chords you are playing over, it may sound best to start on **any** of the notes in the scale. E.g. if you were playing over a **C** chord followed by a **D minor** chord you could play the scale starting on **C** for the **C chord** but start on **D** for the **D minor** chord, as shown in the following example. This is a **modal** approach to playing scales, which is the way Jazz players often use scales.

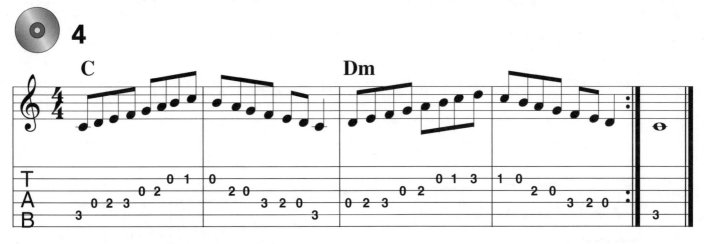

As well as knowing which notes will sound best over a particular chord, the things which make a melody interesting are the rhythm and the order the notes are played in. The scale is only the starting point. If you just run up and down a scale, it gets boring very quickly. Compare the following example with the previous one and you will hear how a melody can be created from the scale. This melody is played with a **swing feel**, which will be discussed in following lessons.

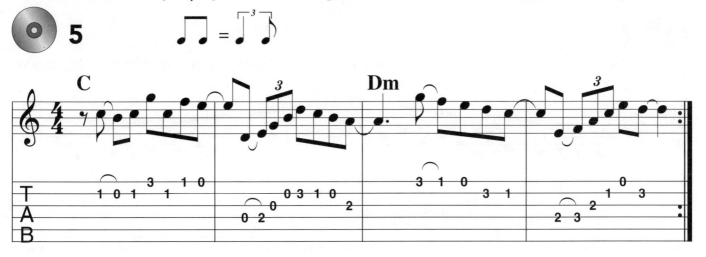

CREATING YOUR OWN MELODIES

In order to create melodies like the one in the previous example, you need to have a working knowledge of several things apart from the scale itself. These include **rhythm**, **harmony** and **intervals**, along with the ability to hear sounds in your mind before you play them and the technique to reproduce these sounds on your instrument. All these things will be covered in the course of the book.

SEQUENCES

One of the best ways to practice scales is the use of sequences. A **sequence** is a repetitive pattern in which the rhythm remains the same while the pitches are repeated higher or lower, usually within a specific scale or key. Practicing sequences will help you to become more familiar with the scale you are learning as well as enabling you to create melodies more easily instead of just running up and down the scale. Here are some sequences within the C major scale.

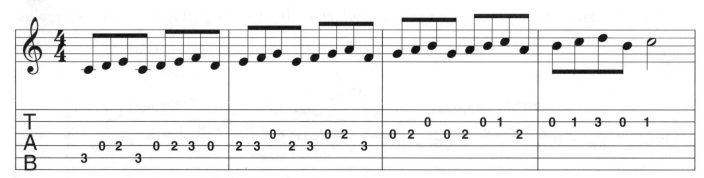

This sequence uses intervals of a 3rd. Intervals will be discussed in detail later in the book.

MEMORIZING THE NOTES OF THE SCALE

In Jazz, the major scale is usually broken up into different **modes** (scales) beginning on each individual note of the scale. Using modes to play over chord progressions means finding the best group of notes to play over each particular chord. There are **seven** different notes in a major scale and each of these notes can be used as the starting note for a different mode. Modes will be explained in detail later in the book. Here is an exercise to help you become familiar with the positions of all of the notes within the open position fingering of the C major scale. These are the starting notes for the seven modes, so it is important to be able to find them all instantly.

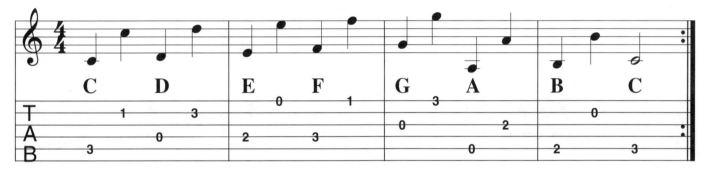

Once you are comfortable finding all the notes individually, practice playing all the notes in between them from one octave to the next as shown in the following example. Once you can do them ascending, practice them descending as well.

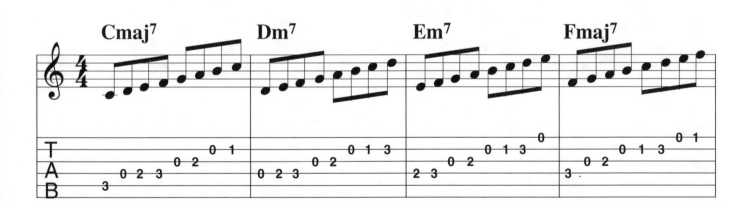

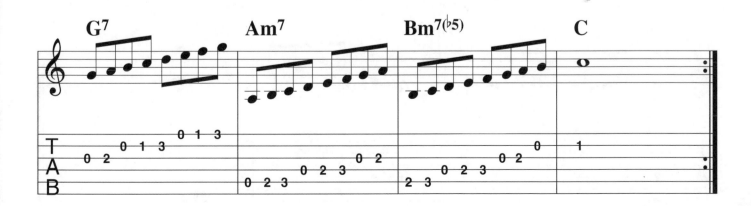

CHORD SYMBOLS

If you look at example 10 (below) you will notice a line of letters and symbols above the staff (**Cmaj7**, **Dm7** etc.) These are **chord symbols** which indicate the harmony to be played by accompanying instruments such as keyboard or another guitar. In section 2 you will learn more about chords and how to play over each chord type.

 10   Headstart

Here is a simple solo derived from the notes of the C major scale. Learn it from memory and then experiment with the ideas and note sequences to create your own melodies. Try improvising with the backing on the accompanying CD. If you have trouble with any of the rhythms, listen to the CD to hear how they should sound and then imitate what you hear. Rhythms will be covered in detail in the following lessons.

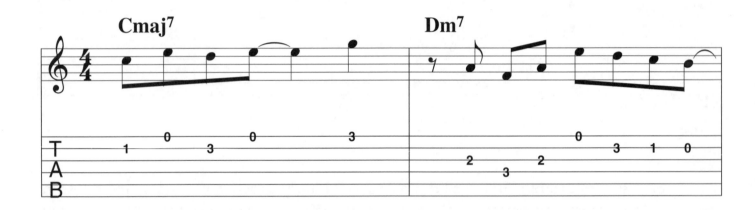

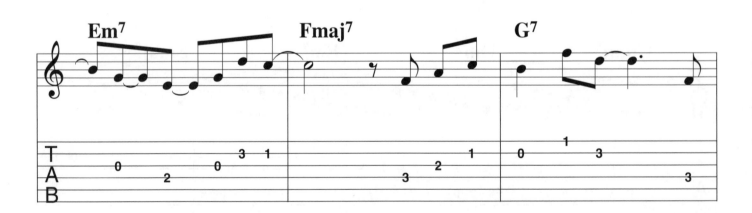

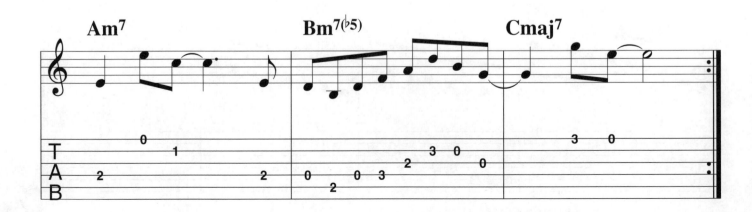

LESSON TWO

UNDERSTANDING RHYTHMS

Regardless of the style of music you play, it is essential to have a good knowledge of rhythms and the note and rest values used to create them. All players use the same notes, but it is largely the control of timing, rhythms and phrasing which separates the great players from the average. There are thousands of licks and solos on albums which use only a few notes (e.g. the notes of the major scale) but are made interesting by the rhythm with which those notes are played. The table below shows whole, half, quarter and eighth notes, along with their equivalent rests. You may already know these values, but it is worth reminding yourself how the notes divide into two each time you go to a smaller note value.

NOTE AND REST VALUES

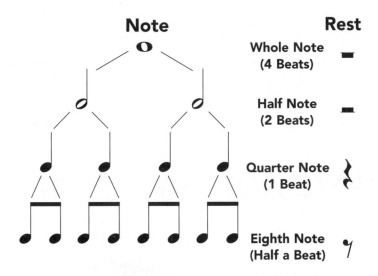

Note   **Rest**

Whole Note (4 Beats)

Half Note (2 Beats)

Quarter Note (1 Beat)

Eighth Note (Half a Beat)

Bar lines are drawn across the staff, which divides the music into sections called **Bars** or **Measures**. A **Double bar line** signifies either the end of the music, or the end of an important section of it.

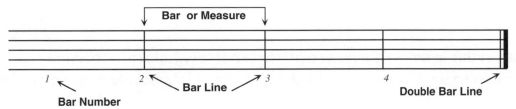

Bar or Measure

1 *2* Bar Line *3* *4* Double Bar Line

Bar Number

THE FOUR FOUR TIME SIGNATURE

 These two numbers are called the **four four time signature.**
They are placed after the treble clef.
The 4/4 time signature tells you there are four beats in each bar.
There are **four** quarter notes in one bar of music in 4/4 time.

THE WHOLE NOTE AND WHOLE REST

 This is a **whole note**. It lasts for **four** beats. There is **one** whole note in one bar of $\frac{4}{4}$ time.

Count: **1** 2 3 4

This symbol is called a **whole rest**. It indicates either **four** beats of silence or a **whole bar** of silence.

Count: 1 2 3 4

In the following example, the guitar plays a whole note in one bar and nothing in the following bar (a whole rest). This means there is a lot of space for the other instruments. Remember to keep counting regardless of whether you see notes or rests in the music. Listen to the CD to hear how the guitar part interacts with the other instruments.

11

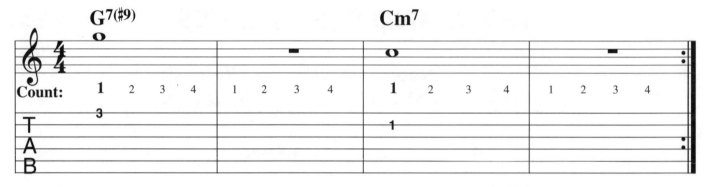

THE HALF NOTE AND HALF REST

 This is a **half note**. It has a value of **two** beats. There are **two** half notes in one bar of $\frac{4}{4}$ time.

Count: **1** 2

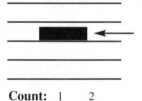

Count: 1 2

12

The guitar part in this example makes use of whole notes, whole rests, half notes and half rests. Once again, listen to the CD to hear how the guitar part interacts with the other instruments.

THE QUARTER NOTE AND QUARTER REST

 This is a **quarter note**. It lasts for **one** beat. There are **four** quarter notes in one bar of $\frac{4}{4}$ time.

This symbol is a **quarter rest.** It indicates **one beat of silence**. Do not play any note. Small counting numbers are placed under rests.

Count: 1

Count: 1

 13

This example demonstrates quarter notes and quarter rests. As with previous examples, listen to the CD to hear the interaction between the guitar part and the other instruments.

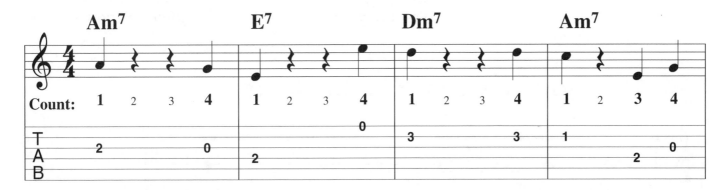

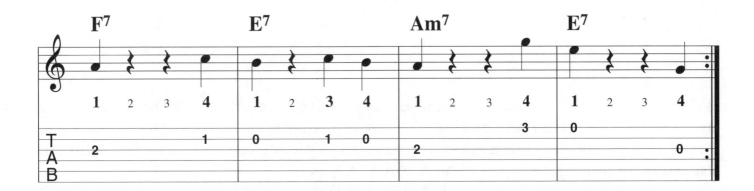

THE IMPORTANCE OF TIMING AND ATTITUDE

One of the most important attributes of any great singer or instrumentalist is great timing and phrasing. This means they have developed the ability to begin and end a note or phrase at precisely the right moment and to fit their playing in with the accompaniment for maximum musical and dramatic effect. To develop a good time feel right from the start, you should always practice with a metronome or drum machine if you are not playing with other musicians. Great players also mean every note, nothing is unconvincing or half-hearted. A good example of this is the bass player in a Jazz group. Walking basslines often consist mainly of "simple" quarter notes. A great player can drive the whole group with the way they play these quarter notes. It is the feeling and attitude the notes are played with that makes all the difference. Once you can play something, you must be totally committed to it. Never think "this is easy, I don't really need to concentrate here", or this attitude will become a part of your playing. **Good players make simple things sound great**, and this is what you should strive for right from the start. Treat everything you play as **music**, rather than having one attitude for "exercises" and another for "real music".

LESSON THREE

EIGHTH NOTES

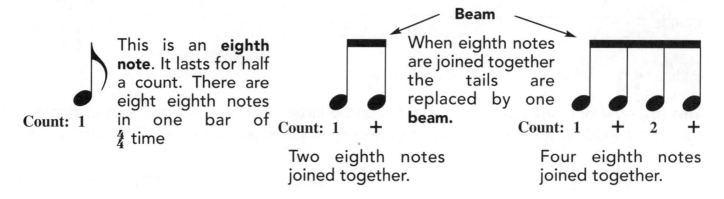

This is an **eighth note**. It lasts for half a count. There are eight eighth notes in one bar of $\frac{4}{4}$ time

Count: 1

When eighth notes are joined together the tails are replaced by one **beam**.

Beam

Count: 1 +

Two eighth notes joined together.

Count: 1 + 2 +

Four eighth notes joined together.

14   How to Count Eighth Notes

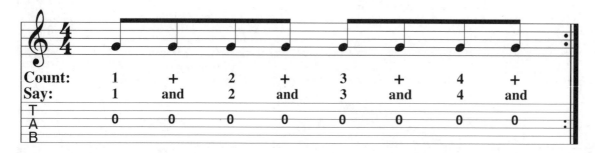

When playing eighth notes, a combination of down (V) and up (Λ) picking is commonly used. This is called **alternate picking**. Using it consistently will increase the smoothness, speed and accuracy of your playing. The following example contains all eighth notes, so use alternate picking, i.e.

V Λ V Λ V Λ V Λ
1 + 2 + 3 + 4 +

Use a down pick on the beat (the number count) and an up pick off the beat (the "and" + count).

 15

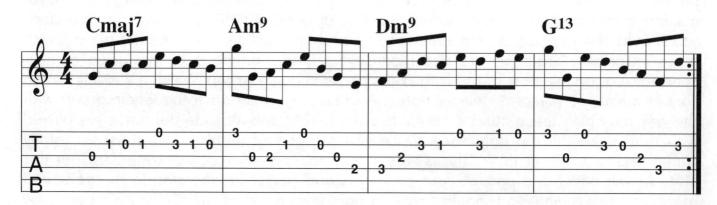

When you use eighth notes, there are many more rhythmic possibilities than when using whole, half and quarter notes. For this reason it is a good idea to have a systematic approach to gaining control of eighth notes. To begin with, try playing through the C major scale using a quarter note on the first beat of the bar and eighth notes for the rest of the bar, as shown in the example below.

USING SET RHYTHMS

Once you can play the scale in this manner at a reasonably quick tempo without losing the rhythm, try memorizing the rhythm on one note first, and then improvising with it. Play any notes from the scale in any order you like, but be sure to keep the rhythm exactly the same every bar. Don't worry if your melodies don't sound great at first, as your ear and your musical knowledge develops, improvising will become easier and easier. The following example demonstrates four bars of an improvised melody using this set rhythm.

The next step is to move the quarter note to the second beat and play eighth notes in the rest of the bar. Once again, memorize the rhythm and then improvise with it. Then repeat the process with the quarter note on the third beat of the bar, and then again on the fourth beat of the bar. Each of these rhythms is shown on one note in the example below, along with the rhythm from the previous example.

LESSON FOUR

MORE ABOUT EIGHTH NOTES

There is a simple system for identifying any note's position in a bar by naming notes off the beat according to which beat they come directly after. The system works as follows. Within a bar of continuous eighth notes in 4/4 time, there are **eight** possible places where notes could occur. The first beat is called **one** (1), the next eighth note is called the "**and of one**", then comes beat **two**, the next eighth note is called the "**and of two**", then beat **three**, followed by the "**and of three**", then beat **four**, followed by the "**and of four**" which is the final eighth note in the bar. These positions are shown in the notation below.

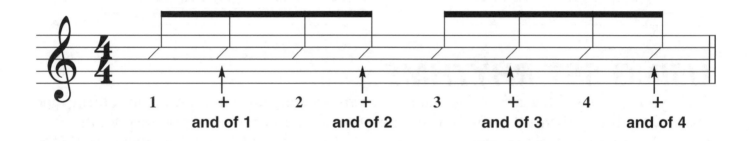

1	+	2	+	3	+	4	+
	and of 1		and of 2		and of 3		and of 4

THE EIGHTH REST

This symbol is an **eighth rest.** It indicates **half a beat** of silence.

When improvising melodies, where you choose not to play notes is as important as where you do play notes. The following example contains an eighth rest on the first two beats of each bar. Listen to the CD and notice how this allows space for the rhythm section to be heard.

 18

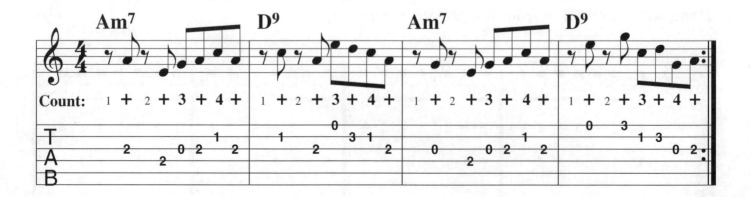

SYNCOPATION

A good way to become more comfortable with eighth rests is to play a scale with a rhythm pattern containing an eighth rest on every beat and an eighth note in between every beat, which creates a syncopated rhythm. **Syncopation** means displacing the normal flow of accents, usually from on the beat to off the beat. This is demonstrated in the following example. When using rests, counting is particularly important so you don't get lost and play notes in the wrong place.

 19

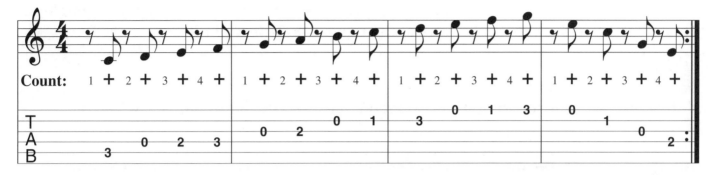

Now try improvising with set rhythms which contain eighth rests. As mentioned earlier, it is best to memorize the rhythm on one note first, and then to improvise with it. Here are some examples of this type of playing. Remember to use the system shown on the previous page to identify where the notes fall in relation to the four beats of the bar.

 20

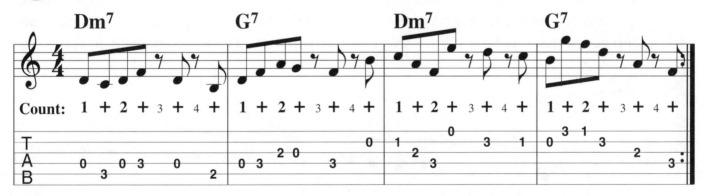

 21

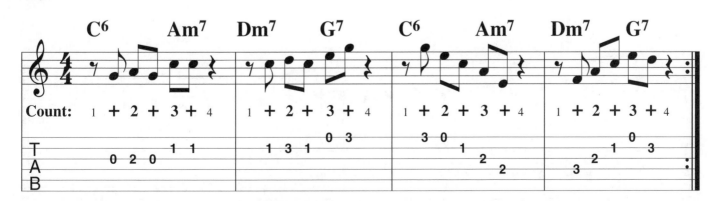

LESSON FIVE

THE TRIPLET

Count 1 trip let

A **triplet** is a group of **three** evenly spaced notes played within one beat. Eighth note triplets are indicated by three eighth notes grouped together by a bracket (or a curved line) and the numeral **3**. Each note has the value of one third of a beat. Triplets are easy to understand once you have heard them played. Listen to example 22 on the CD to hear the effect of triplets.

 22

Notice the different sound used for counting each part of the triplet: **1 – trip – let**.

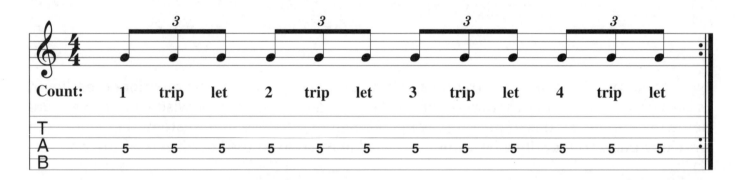

Once you are comfortable playing triplets on one note, try running through a scale with them, and then play some sequences based on triplets, as shown in the following example. Use alternate picking and notice that one beat starts with a downstroke, while the next starts with an upstroke.

 23

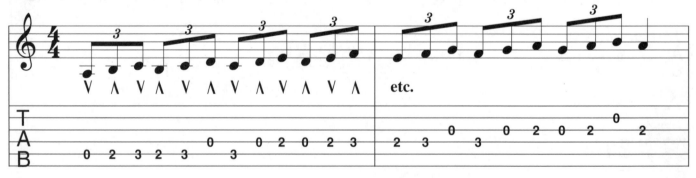

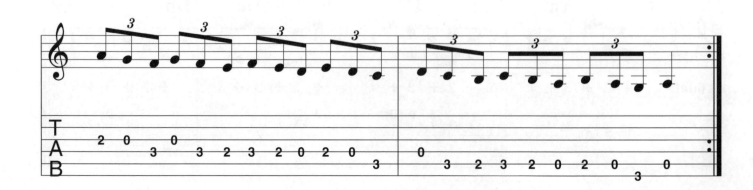

SWING RHYTHMS

A **swing rhythm** can be created by tying the first two notes of the triplet group together.

 24.0

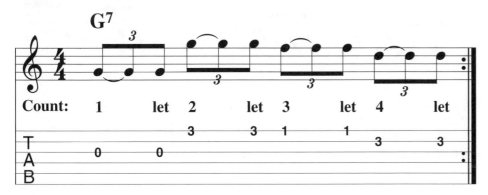

 24.1

The two eighth note triplets tied together in example 28 can be replaced by a quarter note.

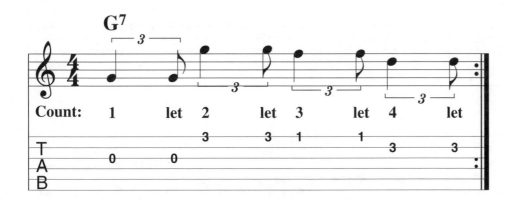

To simplify notation, it is common to replace the ♪ ♪ with ♪♪ ,
and to write at the start of the piece ♪♪ = ♪ ♪ as illustrated below in example 24.1.

24.2

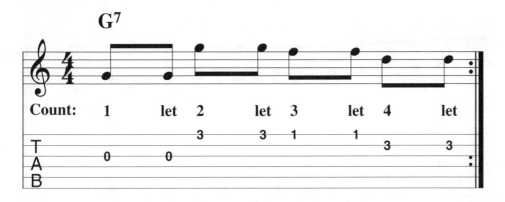

To play Jazz well, it is essential to have good control of playing swing 8th notes, as they are the most common rhythmic used in Jazz. Practice the following sequence using swing 8ths until you can play it smoothly and evenly at a reasonable tempo **without** accenting the notes on the beat.

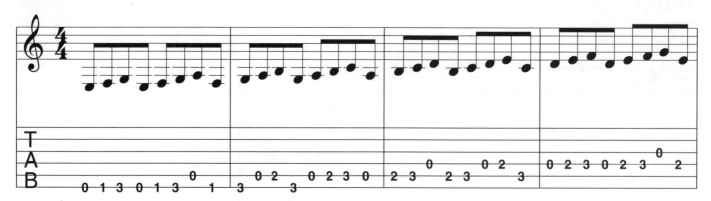

COUNTING SWING EIGHTH NOTES

When playing swing eighth notes, it is easier to count them as eighth notes rather than triplet subdivisions: i.e. count them **1 and 2 and 3 and 4 and**, with each "**and**" being half as long as the note on the beat. Try playing through the scale from **C** to **C ascending**, **D** to **D descending**, **E** to **E ascending**, etc. using swing eighth notes as shown below and count as you play.

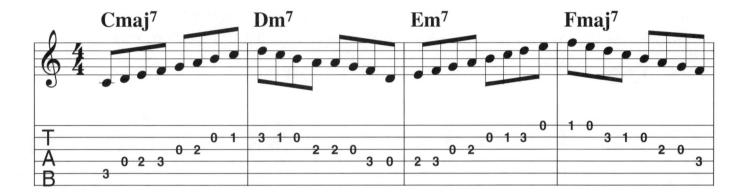

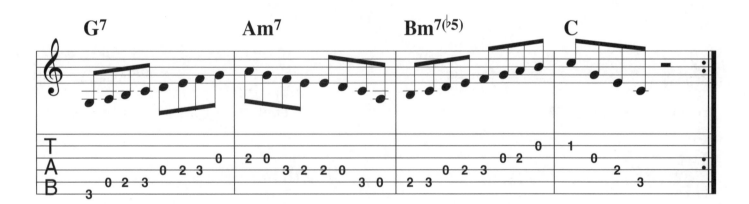

Once you start to feel comfortable using swing eighth notes, try improvising with them. Start with some set rhythms by adding rests or other note values. The following example uses a rest on the first beat of the bar.

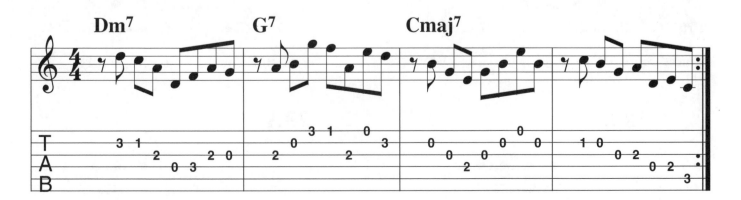

LESSON SIX

DEVELOPING RHYTHMIC CONTROL

To become a good Jazz player, it is essential to have control over exactly where in the bar you play and where you don't play. A good way to develop this ability is to concentrate totally on rhythm by using only one note and to play it in all different rhythmic positions within a bar. The following examples begin with a pair of eighth notes played on each beat of the bar and then move on to groups of four notes played in various different positions. It is important to count as you play the following examples and try to memorize each one.

28.0

Count   1   +   2   3   4

28.1

Count   1   2   +   3   4

28.2

Count   1   3   3   +   4

28.3

Count   1   2   3   4   +

28.4

Count   1   +   2   +   3   4

28.5

Count   1   +   2   +   3   +   4

28.6

Count   1   2   +   3   +   4

28.7

Count   1   2   +   3   +   4   +

28.8
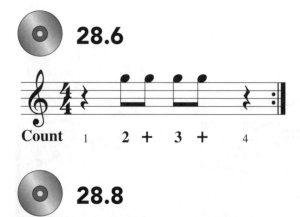

Count   1   2   3   +   4   +

28.9
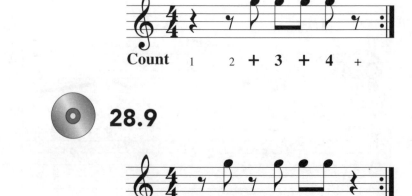

Count   1   +   2   +   3   +   4

IMPROVISING WITH SET RHYTHMS

The next step is to play these short rhythm figures between different pitches to create melodies, and eventually to improvise with the rhythms. The idea is that you can play any pitches you like, but the rhythm remains the same every bar. The following example uses the rhythm from example 28.9 played on various pitches derived from the C major scale.

29

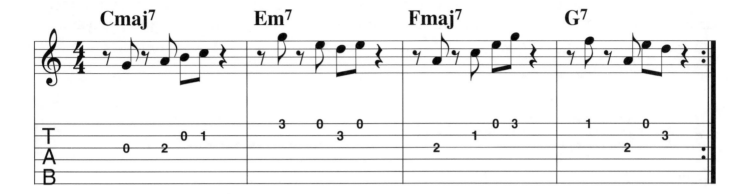

Here is a set rhythm example which uses swing eighth note rhythms covering **two bars**. The rhythm is shown first on one note and then as a melody using various pitches. Create some of your own two bar rhythms and use them to improvise with.

30.0

30.1

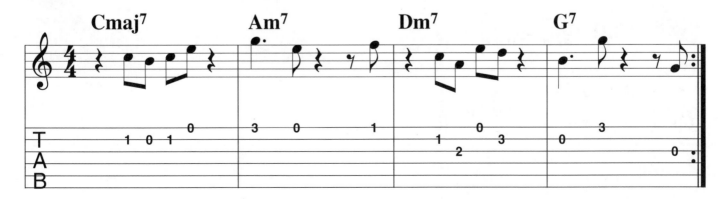

LESSON SEVEN

USING TIES

A common way of creating syncopated rhythms is by using **ties**. The following example shows a rhythm played in the first bar using eighth notes and a half note. In the second bar, the half note is tied to the last eighth note creating a syncopated rhythm. Once again, **count** as you play all examples and always use a metronome or drum machine when you practice as it is essential to develop a good sense of time if you wish to become a good player.

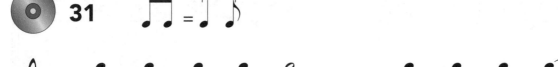

A good way to gain control of syncopated rhythms using ties is to play a scale as shown in the following example. After the first note, all of the notes on the beat are tied, which means each new note occurs off the beat.

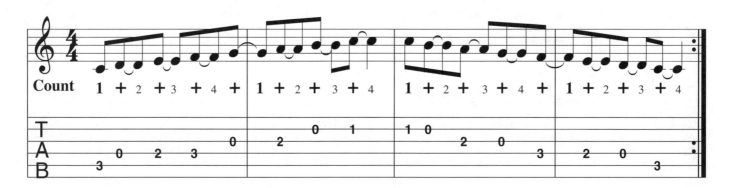

Here is an example of a set rhythm using a tie. The rhythm is given first on one note and then as the basis for a melody.

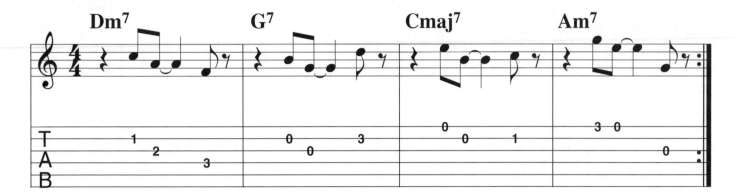

Here are two more syncopated rhythms created by the use of ties. Try making up some of your own. Play them on one note at first and then try improvising with them. Once you are comfortable with one bar rhythms, try some which repeat every two bars.

TIES ACROSS A BAR LINE

The following example demonstrates the use of ties both within a bar and across bar lines. The use of a tie is the only way of indicating that a note is to be held across a bar line.

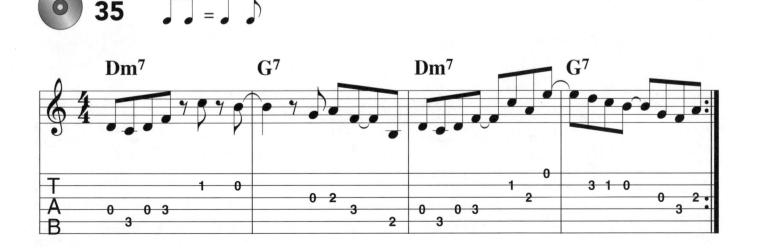

FIRST AND SECOND ENDINGS

To finish this section, here is a solo which makes use of everything you have learned up to this point. Learn it from memory and practice it along with the CD. You should also experiment with the rhythms and phrases from the solo to create your own ideas and improvise with them. By now you should be improvising as part of your daily practice. This solo begins with three **lead-in** (or pickup) notes, which are notes that occur before the first full bar. When a lead-in or pickup is used, the final bar of the section is also incomplete. The notes in the lead-in and the final bar add up to one full bar. The solo also contains first and second endings.The **first** time you play through the song, play the **first ending** ([1.   ]), then go back to the beginning. The **second** time you play through the song, play the **second ending** ([2.   ]) instead of the first.

 36   **Changing Seasons**

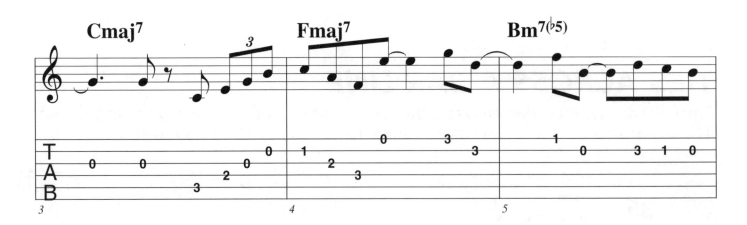

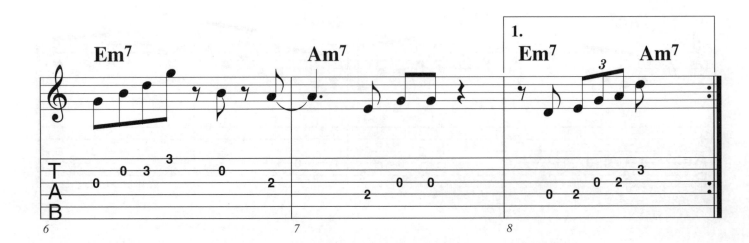

SECTION 2

Using the Whole Fretboard, Playing in all Keys

LESSON EIGHT

SCALE DEGREES

So far, everything you have learnt has related to the C major scale in the open position. However, in order to become a good Jazz player, you will need to be able to play in all keys in any position on the fretboard. To do this, you need a system for identifying pitches which can apply to any scale in any key. The easiest way to do this is to use **scale degrees** to identify a note's position in the scale in relation to the **keynote** (the note after which the key is named – also called the **tonic**).

Here are the notes of the **C major scale** with the scale degrees written under the notes. Try playing the scale and singing the scale degree numbers as you play. It is important to learn scale degrees well because a good knowledge of them is essential for transposing music to other keys and for playing effectively over chord progressions.

C	D	E	F	G	A	B	C
1	2	3	4	5	6	7	8

Keynote or Tonic

VISUALIZING SCALE DEGREES

The diagram below shows the fretboard pattern for the **C major scale** in the open position with the scale degrees written in. Practice running through the whole pattern **with your eyes closed**, visualizing the fretboard in your mind and naming the degrees as you go. Once you can do this easily, try finding various degrees at random until you can do it instantly. Finally, practice improvising melodies with your eyes closed, stopping suddenly and naming the degree you finished on. Keep working on this until you can do it easily.

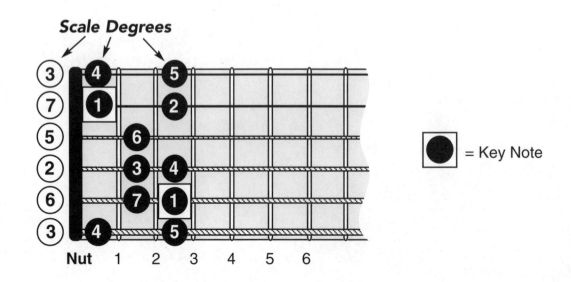

Scale Degrees

● = Key Note

Nut   1   2   3   4   5   6

5 FORMS OF MOVEABLE FINGERINGS

For any scale there are five basic moveable fingering patterns which can be moved to any part of the fretboard. These fingerings can be named according to the chord shape to which each fingering corresponds. The names of the five forms (formations or patterns) are easy to memorize because they spell the word **CAGED** when put together. It is the position of the keynotes in each fingering which determines the name of the form. End to end these five forms cover the whole fretboard before repeating. The fingerings of these forms are shown below for the **C major scale** along with the chord shapes to which they relate.

Open Chord Shape	Chord Form	Major Scale Form

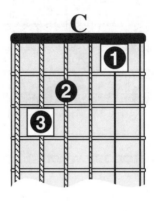

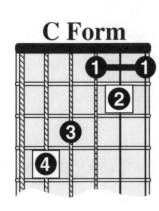

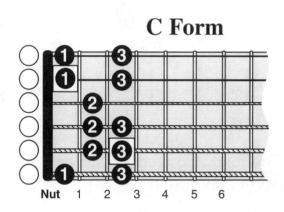

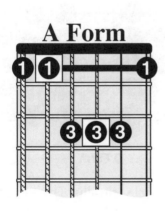

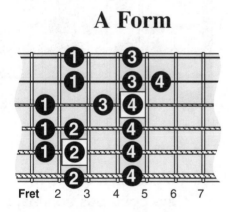

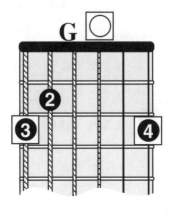

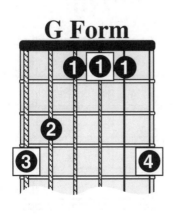

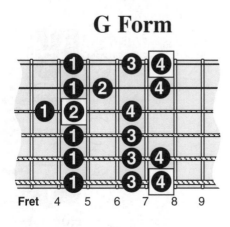

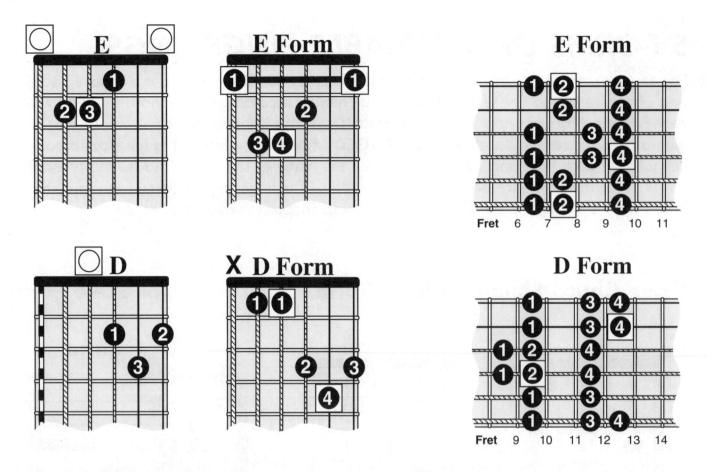

The following diagram shows how the five forms cover the whole fretboard when placed end to end.

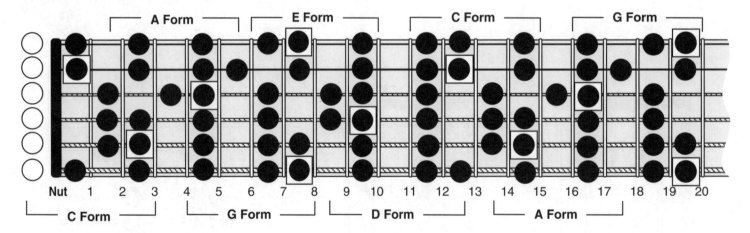

Let's look at each of the five scale forms individually. The diagram below shows the **C form**. This is the open position major scale you learnt in section 1.

C Form

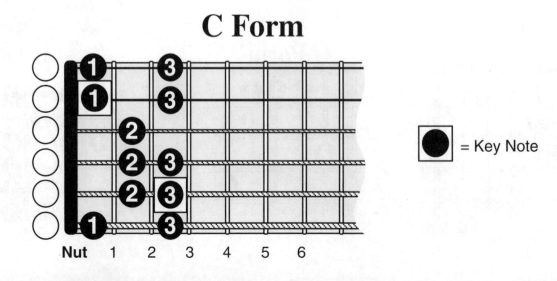

● = Key Note

Here are the other four forms. Learn them one at a time and practice them until you can play them all from memory. **It is particularly important to memorize the positions of the key notes in each form**, as they are like landmarks which you can always refer back to.

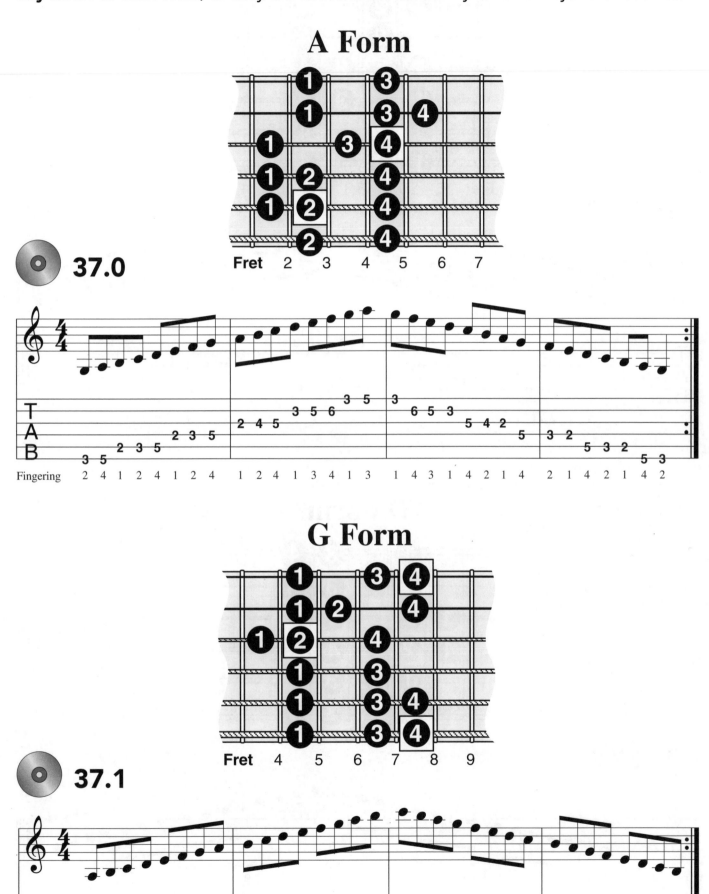

E Form

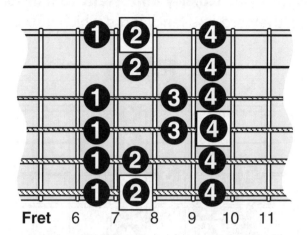

37.2

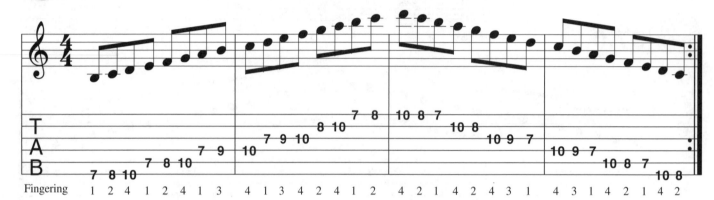

D Form

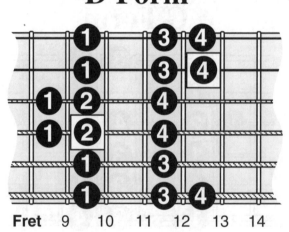

37.3

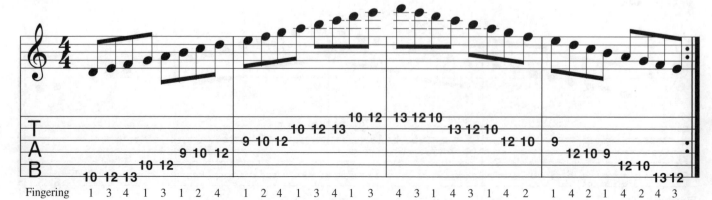

LESSON NINE

Progressing still higher up the fretboard, here is the **C form an octave higher** than the open position C form. At this point the pattern of five forms begins to repeat.

C Form

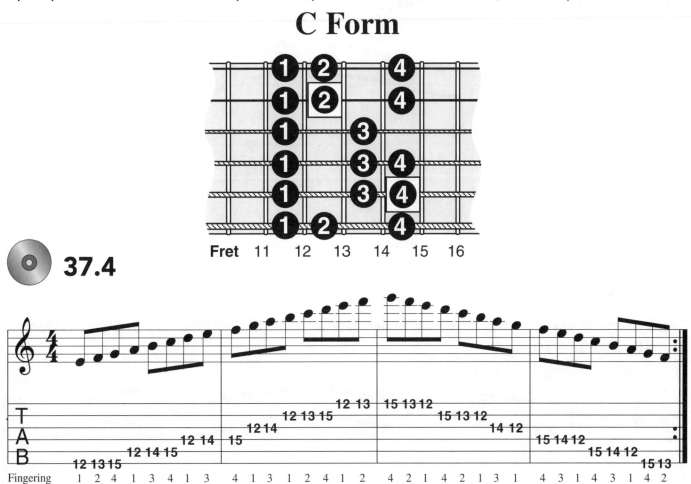

37.4

You have now learnt all five forms of the C major scale. Because each of these fingerings is moveable, it is possible to play them in any key. All you need to do is to locate the **root note** (key note) and then follow the correct fingering. E.g. once you know that the root notes for a **C form** scale are always on the **5th and 2nd strings**, you just find the note of the key you wish to play in on either of those strings. The example below shows the moveable **C form** fingering of the **D major scale**, which is in the second position. The fretboard "position" is determined by the fret your **first finger** is at: i.e. in the **second position**, your first finger is at the **second fret**.

38

38

 39

Here is the **E form** of the **A major scale**. The **E form** can always be identified by the root notes on the **6th, 4th and 1st strings**.

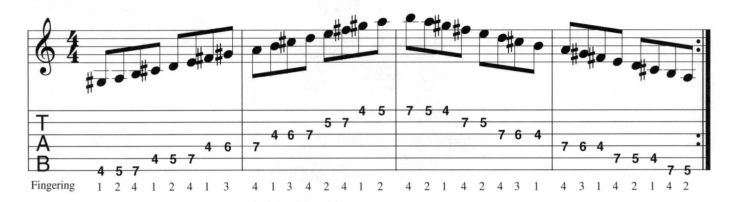

 40

Here is the **D form** of the **G major scale**. The **D form** is identified by the root notes on the **4th and 2nd strings**.

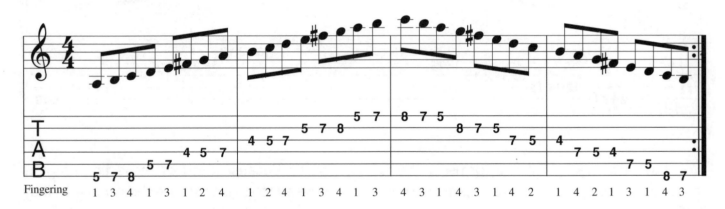

 41

This example shows the **A form** of the **F major scale**. The **A form** is identified by the root notes on the **5th and 3rd strings**.

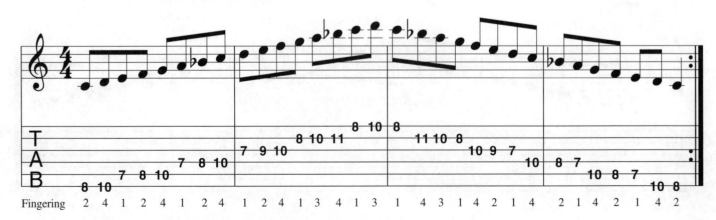

Once you know the fingering for each scale form, practice each one using various sequence patterns as shown in the following examples. This first one uses the **A form of C major**.

42.0

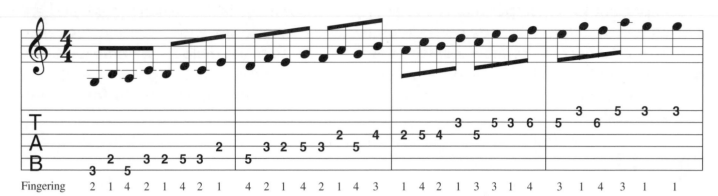

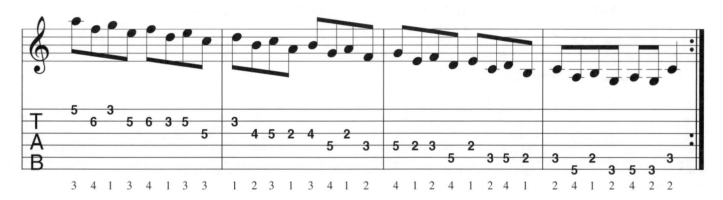

42.1

The following example shows a triplet sequence played in the **G form of C major**.

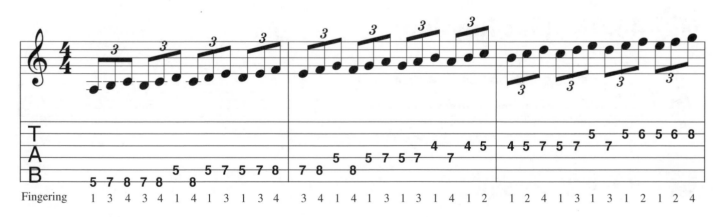

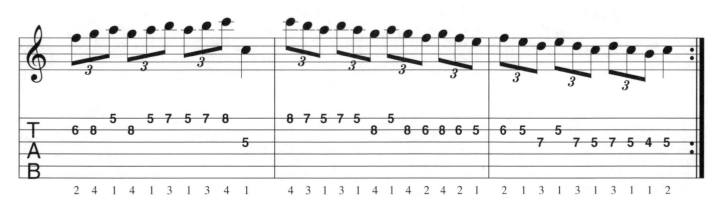

LESSON TEN

USING THE SCALE FORMS

It is important to remember that scales are just the raw material for making music and are not an end in themselves. The purpose of learning all the forms and practicing sequence patterns is to become comfortable with them in order to make melodic statements. Once you are confident with the scale forms, you should practice improvising within each one as part of your daily practice. Here is an example of a line derived from the **A form** of the **C major scale**.

43

If you are having trouble playing lines within the different forms, try using some set rhythms until you are comfortable using all the notes of each form. Here is an example which uses the **E form** of C major.

44.0   (Set Rhythm)

44.1

PLAYING WHAT YOU HEAR

Another important aspect of understanding the scale forms is being able to play what you hear in your mind, and to play the same thing in many different places on the fretboard. Once you can play whatever you hear in any of the five forms, the need to move to somewhere "more comfortable" is eliminated and you can improvise much more freely.

A good way to develop this ability is to play a simple melody you already know from memory (e.g. Yankee Doodle) in any of the forms, and then move it to all other possible fingerings on the fretboard. You can often play the same melody twice in different octaves within the one form. Once you can easily play a melody anywhere on the fretboard, choose another one and repeat the process, then another, etc. Make it part of your daily practice. As you progress, you will be able to do this with more sophisticated lines, but start with simple ones.

The following example shows a two bar phrase played in all five forms in the key of **C major**.

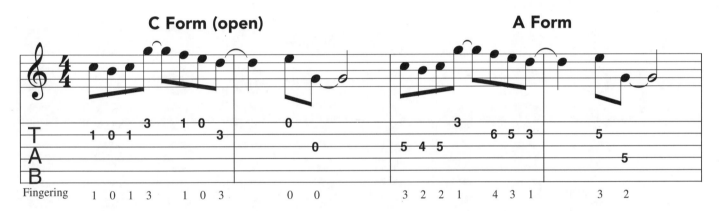

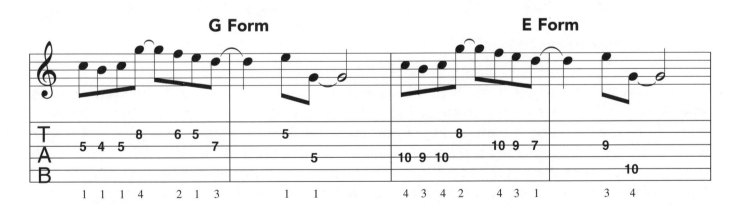

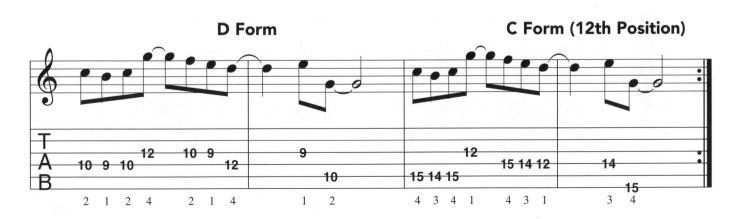

LESSON ELEVEN

LEARNING ALL THE NOTES

When using moveable scale or chord forms, it is important to be able to quickly find the correct fret at which to play each note and also to be able to play equally well in all keys. The best way to achieve this is to memorize the names of all the notes on the fretboard. Jazz guitar uses many different scales and chords which may take their name from **any** of the six strings, so be sure to learn them all equally well. Shown below is a diagram containing all of the notes on the guitar fretboard up to the 19th fret.

Notes on the

Here is a fretboard diagram of all the notes on the guitar. Play the notes on each string from the the open 6th string is an **E** note and the note on the 12th fret of the 6th string is also an **E** note,

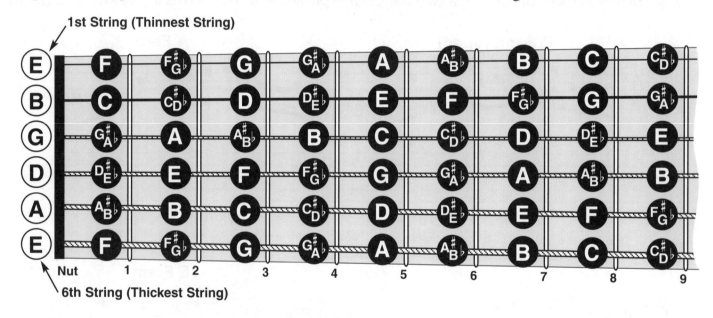

A good way to learn all the notes is to take one string at a time. Call the "in between" notes sharps as you progress up the fretboard and flats as you go back down. Shown below is a diagram of the notes on the 4th string. To practice naming the notes, slide your first finger up one fret at a time and say the name of each note out loud as you go. When you reach the 12th fret where the notes repeat, move back down one fret at a time. You can use any finger to do this exercise, it is the note names that are important here, not the fingering.

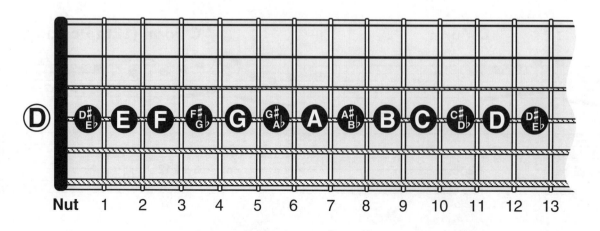

The dots on your guitar are good points of reference. You can use them to help the memorizing process.

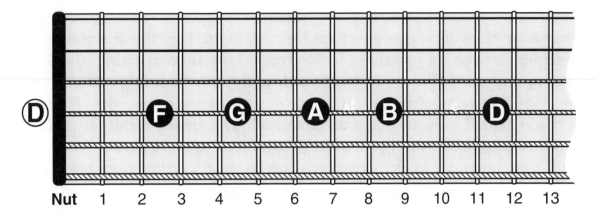

Guitar Fretboard

open notes to the 12th fret. The note on the 12th fret is one octave higher than the open note e.g. but is one octave higher.

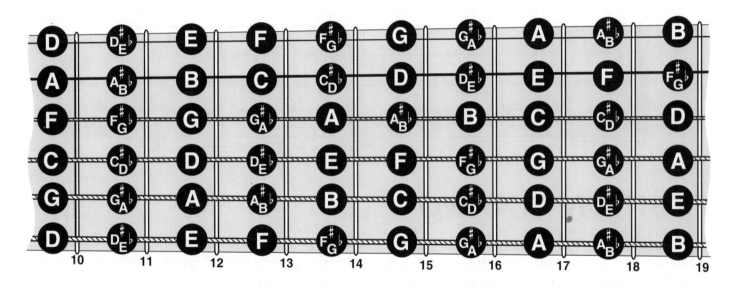

Once you are confident you know the names of the notes along a particular string, pick the name of any note at random and find it as quickly as possible. When this becomes easy, move on to the next string.

Another useful exercise is to find the same note on every string. Usually a note appears twice on each string unless it is at the 11th fret.

One last way to learn the notes is to name them across each fret. Once again use sharps as you go higher in pitch and flats as you go back down.

NOTES IN MORE THAN ONE PLACE

Once you start playing notes all over the fretboard, you quickly realize that you can find the same notes in more than one place on the fretboard. E.g. the **E note** which is the **open first string** can also be found at the **5th fret** on the **second string**, the **9th fret** on the **third string** and the **14th fret** on the **fourth string** (on electric guitars it can also be found at the **19th fret** on the **fifth string**). Once you are comfortable with all the locations of a note, this makes it easy to play the same melody in many different places on the fretboard, which is valuable when you are improvising or reading music. Practice naming any note and then finding it in as many places on the fretboard as possible. Keep doing this for a few minutes each day until you are confident you can quickly find all the locations for any note.

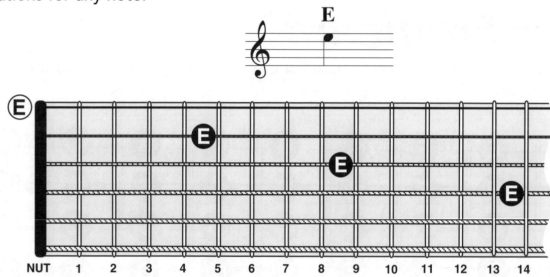

POSITION PLAYING

A valuable way of looking at the notes on the guitar fretboard is to think in terms of **positions**. The position you are playing is determined by which fret the **first finger** of your left hand is at. E.g. if you are playing a melody or chord where your first finger stays at the **first fret**, then you are in the **first position**. If your first finger stays at the **6th fret**, you are in the **6th position**, etc. The example below demonstrates a short phrase in played in several different positions, as shown in the tablature. Experiment and find out how many other positions you can use to play this phrase.

 46

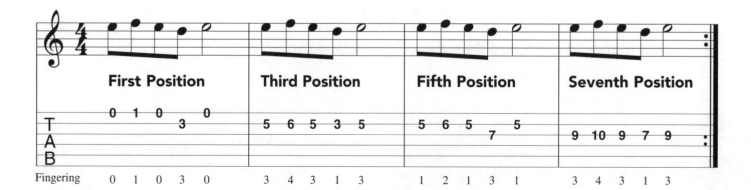

HIGHER AND LOWER VERSIONS OF NOTES

Another valuable exercise for improving your knowledge of the fretboard is to find all possible versions (i.e. higher and lower pitches) of any given note. An example of this would be the note **C#** which can be found at the **9th and 21st frets** on the **sixth string**, the **4th and 16th frets** on the **fifth string**, the **11th fret** on the **fourth string**, the **6th and 18th frets** on the **third string**, the **2nd and 14th frets** on the **second string**, and the **9th and 21st frets** on the **first string**. These positions are shown in the diagram below. Practice choosing notes at random and finding each one in all possible positions until you are confident you can instantly find any note in any position.

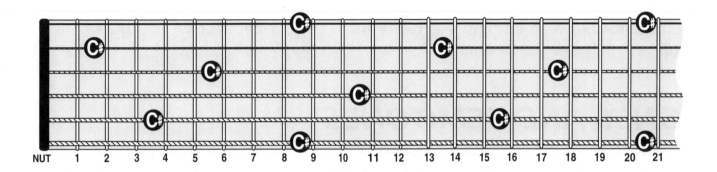

Knowing how to find higher and lower versions of notes is useful in many ways. You may wish to repeat something you have played but make it sound higher or lower than the first time it was played, or you may play something and think you have the right notes but it sounds too high or too low. Another situation where this is useful is if you are playing call and response with a vocalist or another instrumentalist. You may know which key they are in and what note they are starting with, but you have to find which octave they are in as well. An **octave** is the distance between any note and its next repeat at a higher or lower pitch. The example below shows a phrase played in different positions on the fretboard and also in different octaves.

47

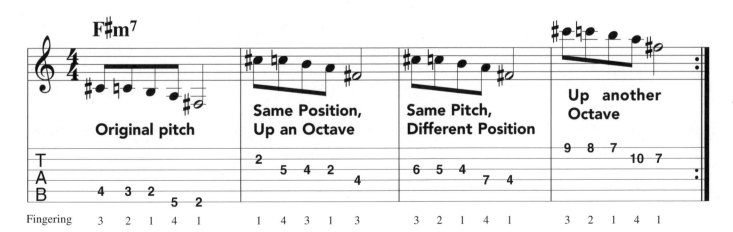

LESSON TWELVE

MORE ABOUT MAJOR SCALES

The **C major scale** contains the following notes.

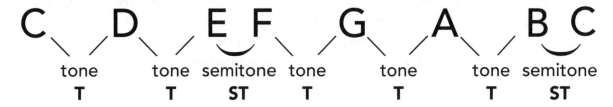

C D E F G A B C

tone	tone	semitone	tone	tone	tone	semitone
T	T	ST	T	T	T	ST

The distance between each note is two frets (a tone) except for **EF** and **BC** where the distance is only one fret (a semitone).

TONES AND SEMITONES

A **semitone** is the smallest distance between two notes used in western music. On the guitar, notes which are a semitone apart are **one fret** apart, (e.g. the note **C** on the 3rd fret 5th string is one semitone above the note **B** at the second fret). This could also be reversed, i.e. the note B is one semitone (one fret) below the note C. Notes which are a **tone** (two semitones) apart, are **two frets** apart. An example of this would be the notes F and G on the sixth string or the first string, or the notes G (open) and A (2nd fret) on the third string.

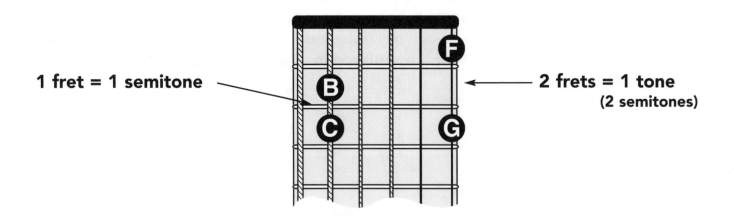

1 fret = 1 semitone

2 frets = 1 tone
(2 semitones)

Here is the pattern of tones and semitones with the scale degrees written under the notes.

Note	C	D	E	F	G	A	B	C
Scale Degree	1	2	3	4	5	6	7	8
Tone Pattern		T	T	ST	T	T	T	ST

T =Tone (2 frets)

ST =Semitone (1 fret)

MAJOR SCALE PATTERN

Once you know the pattern of tones and semitones used to create the C major scale, you can build a major scale on **any** of the twelve notes used in music. It is important to memorize this pattern, which is shown below.

Tone   Tone   Semitone   Tone   Tone   Tone   Semitone

The **semitones** are always found between the **3rd and 4th**, and **7th and 8th** degrees of the scale. All the other notes are a tone apart.

THE G MAJOR SCALE

To demonstrate how the major scale pattern works starting on any note, here is the **G major scale**. Notice that the 7th degree is F sharp (**F♯**) instead of F. This is done to maintain the correct pattern of tones and semitones and thus retain the sound of the major scale (**do re mi fa so la ti do**).

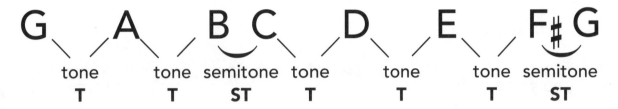

48

No tablature is shown for this example, as **you can play this scale in at least six different places on the fretboard**. Get into the habit of playing everything you learn in as many places as possible.

THE F MAJOR SCALE

By starting the major scale pattern on the note F, it is possible to create an **F major scale**. In this scale, it is necessary to flatten the 4th degree from B to **B♭** to maintain the correct pattern of tones and semitones.

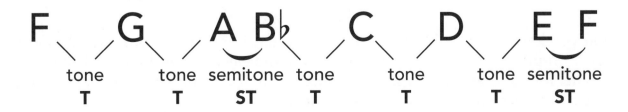

49.0

Here is the F major scale written in standard notation.

OTHER MAJOR SCALES

By simply following the pattern of tones and semitones, it is possible to construct a major scale starting on any note. The scale will be named by the note it starts on. The following example demonstrates several more major scales. **Play them all in the first position and name each note out loud as you play it**. Once you can do this, move each one to as many different places on the fretboard as possible.

D major scale

E major scale

B♭ major scale

A♭ major scale

Now that you know how major scales are constructed, try writing out and playing major scales built on the notes **A, B, F♯, E♭, D♭** and **G♭**. Some will contain sharps, while others will contain flats. Remember that the scale is named from its starting note and all you have to do is follow the pattern of tones and semitones.

LESSON THIRTEEN

KEYS AND KEY SIGNATURES

The **key** describes the note around which a piece of music is built. When a song consists of notes from a particular scale, it is said to be written in the **key** which has the same notes as that scale. For example, if a song contains mostly notes from the **C major scale**, it is said to be in the **key of C major**. If a song contains mostly notes from the **F major scale**, it is said to be in the **key of F major**. If a song contains mostly notes from the **G major scale**, it is said to be in the **key of G major**. When playing in any major key other than C, the key will contain at least one sharp or flat, and possibly as many as six. Instead of writing these sharps or flats before each note as they occur, they are usually written at the beginning of the song just before the time signature. These sharps or flats are called a **key signature**. The number of sharps or flats in the key signature depends on the number of sharps or flats in the corresponding major scale. The major scales and key signatures for the keys of **F** and **G** are shown below. Without sharps and flats, these scales would not contain the correct pattern of tones and semitones and would therefore not sound like a major scale.

G Major Scale

Note	G	A	B	C	D	E	F#	G
Scale Degree	1	2	3	4	5	6	7	8
Tone Pattern		T	T	ST	T	T	T	ST

Key Signature of G Major

The **G major** scale contains one sharp, F#, therefore the key signature for the key of **G major** contains one sharp, F#.

F Major Scale

Note	F	G	A	B♭	C	D	E	F
Scale Degree	1	2	3	4	5	6	7	8
Tone Pattern		T	T	ST	T	T	T	ST

Key Signature of F Major

The **F major** scale contains one flat, B♭, therefore the key signature for the key of **F major** contains one flat, B♭.

The reason some scales contain sharps while others contain flats is that there has to be a separate letter name for each note in the scale. E.g. the G major scale contains F# instead of G♭ even though these two notes are identical in sound. However, if G♭ was used, the scale would contain two notes with the letter name G and no note with the letter name F. This is the reason for choosing to call the note F# in this key. In the key of F major, the note B♭ is chosen instead of A# for the same reason. If A# was used, the scale would contain two notes with the letter name A and no note with the letter name B. The note each major scale starts on will determine how many sharps or flats are found in each key signature because of the necessity for the scale to have the correct pattern of tones and semitones in order to sound right. The charts on the following page contain the key signatures of all the major scales used in music, along with the number of sharps or flats contained in each key. Because there are 12 notes used in music, this means there are 12 possible starting notes for major scales (including sharps and flats). This means that some of the keys will have sharps or flats in their name, e.g. F# major, B♭ major, E♭ major, etc. Keys which contain sharps are called sharp keys and keys which contain flats are called flat keys.

Written below are the key signatures for all the major scales that contain sharps.

Sharps F#   F# C#   F# C# G#   F# C# G# D#   F# C# G# D# A#   F# C# G# D# A# E#

The sharp key signatures are summarised in the table below.

*The new sharp **key** is a fifth interval * higher*

Key	Number of Sharps	Sharp Notes
G	1	F#
D	2	F#, C#
A	3	F#, C#, G#
E	4	F#, C#, G#, D#
B	5	F#, C#, G#, D#, A#,
F#	6	F#, C#, G#, D#, A#, E#

*The new sharp **note** is a fifth interval higher*

Written below are the key signatures for all the major scales that contain flats.

Flats B♭   B♭E♭   B♭E♭A♭   B♭E♭ A♭D♭   B♭E♭ A♭D♭G♭   B♭E♭ A♭D♭G♭C♭

The flat key signatures are summarised in the table below.

*The new flat **key** is a fourth interval higher*

Key	Number of Flats	Flat Notes
F	1	B♭
B♭	2	B♭, E♭
E♭	3	B♭, E♭, A♭
A♭	4	B♭, E♭, A♭, D♭
D♭	5	B♭, E♭, A♭, D♭, G♭,
G♭	6	B♭, E♭, A♭, D♭, G♭, C♭

*The new flat **note** is a fourth interval higher*

* An **interval** is the distance between two notes. Intervals are named by the number of letters they are apart, e.g. C to G is a fifth. Intervals are discussed in detail in lesson 15.

MAJOR SCALES IN ALL KEYS

The following example demonstrates one octave of the major scale ascending and descending in every key. Play the whole exercise in the first position and then in all of the five forms along the fretboard until you can do it easily. Learning scales may not seem as interesting as playing melodies, but a little effort at this stage will pay off very well later on, regardless of the style of music you are playing. Memorize the notes of each scale and then try playing it with your eyes closed while visualizing how the notation for the scale would look. Once you have learnt all the scales, you will be able to read music better, play melodies confidently in any key and be able to improvise in any key much more easily.

50

LESSON FOURTEEN

TRANSPOSING

Transposing (or transposition) means changing the key of a piece of music. This can apply to a scale, a phrase, a short melody, or an entire song. The ability to transpose is an essential skill for all musicians to develop. The easiest way to transpose is to write the **scale degrees** under the original melody and then work out which notes correspond to those scale degrees in the key you want to transpose to. You should work towards being able to do this in your head instantly, without the need for notated scale degrees. Written below is a short melody played in the key of **C** and then transposed to the keys of **F** and **G**. Play through them and notice that the melody sounds the same, but the overall pitch may be higher or lower. Transpose this melody to all other major keys. You should also try this same technique with other tunes you know. The more you do this, the easier it gets, and the better you are at transposing, the easier it will be to play Jazz.

 51.0   Key of C

Scale Degrees   1   6   5   3   2   4   5   6   7   1

 **51.1   Key of F**

Scale Degrees   1   6   5   3   2   4   5   6   7   1

51.2   Key of G

Scale Degrees   1   6   5   3   2   4   6   6   7   1

THE CHROMATIC SCALE

In the previous examples, the melody consists entirely of notes from the major scale. However, many melodies use notes from outside the major scale, particularly in styles such as Blues, Jazz, Rock and Funk. These "outside notes" relate to the chromatic scale starting on the same note as the major scale of the key the music is written in. Therefore, if you have a piece of music in the key of C which contains notes which are not in the C major scale, you can relate these notes to the **C chromatic scale**.

C C#/Db D D#/Eb EF F#/Gb G G#/Ab A A#/Bb BC

ENHARMONIC NOTES

The "in between" notes in the chromatic scale can be described as either sharps or flats. Because of the way scales and chords are constructed, **flats are used more often than sharps**. Here once again is the C chromatic scale with scale degrees written under the notes. The scale degrees written here relate to the natural notes and the flat notes. The sharps are **enharmonic equivalents**, which means they are the same pitch (e.g C#=Db and F#=Gb).

C C#/Db D D#/Eb E F F#/Gb G G#/Ab A A#/Bb B C
1 b2 2 b3 3 4 b5 5 b6 6 b7 7 1

The following diagram shows all the notes in the first position on the guitar fretboard. This is one big chromatic scale starting on the open low **E** note and ending on **G#** or **Ab** on the first string. Notice the notes with two names. Remember that the chromatic scale contains only semitones, which means you can start the scale on any note. Practice running through the entire scale ascending and descending with your eyes closed, naming each note aloud as you play and visualizing what the notation would look like.

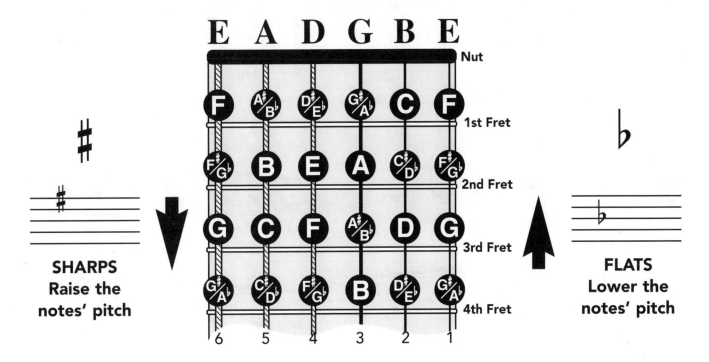

SHARPS
Raise the notes' pitch

FLATS
Lower the notes' pitch

The following example demonstrates a melody in the key of **C** which contains notes from outside the major scale. Once again, no tablature is given for this example. Play it in the first position and then move it through the five forms along the fretboard.

The following examples demonstrate the same melody transposed to the keys of **F** and **G**. Once again, you should transpose it to all the other keys. Before doing this it is worth learning to play the chromatic scale starting on any note. If you do this, it will be easier to play melodies in any key and also make it easier to transpose any melody that you learn in any key.

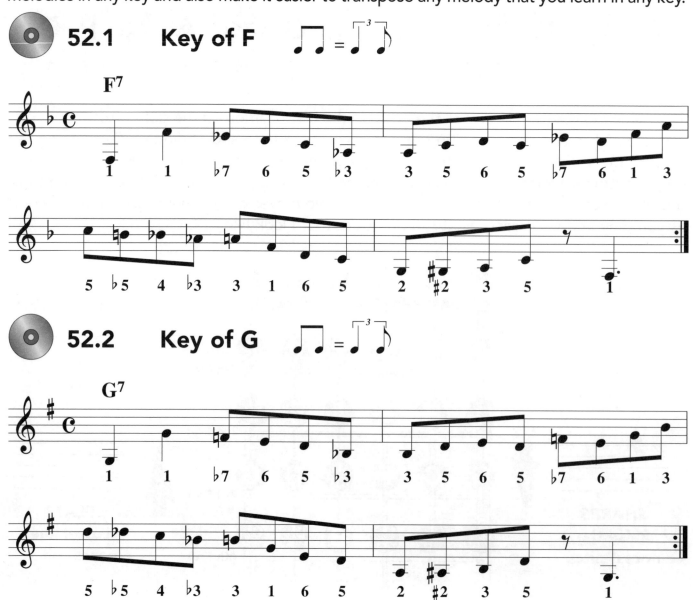

Here are some exercises to help you get more comfortable playing in any key. **Remember to play each one in all possible positions on the fretboard.** Each one is written in a different key, but they are intended to be played in all keys. The first one is a sequence in the key of **D major**.

 **53.0**

 **53.1**

This one alternates between the note **B** and every other note in the **B major scale**, both ascending and descending.

 **53.2**

Don't forget to practice the **chromatic scale** in every key. Here it is in the key of **G♭**.

 **53.3**

Finally, here is one which alternates between the note **A** and every other note in the **A chromatic scale**, once again ascending and descending.

THE KEY CYCLE

There are many reasons why you need to be able to play equally well in every key. Bands often have to play in keys that suit their singer. That could be **F♯** or **D♭** for example. Keyboard players tend to like the keys of **C**, **F** and **G**, while **E** and **A** are fairly common keys for guitar. Horn players like flat keys such as **F**, **B♭** and **E♭**. Apart from this, Jazz tunes often contain many key changes in themselves. For these reasons, you need to learn how keys relate to each other so you can move quickly between them.

One way to do this is to use the **key cycle** (also called the **cycle of 5ths** or **cycle of 4ths**). It contains the names of all the keys and is fairly easy to memorize.

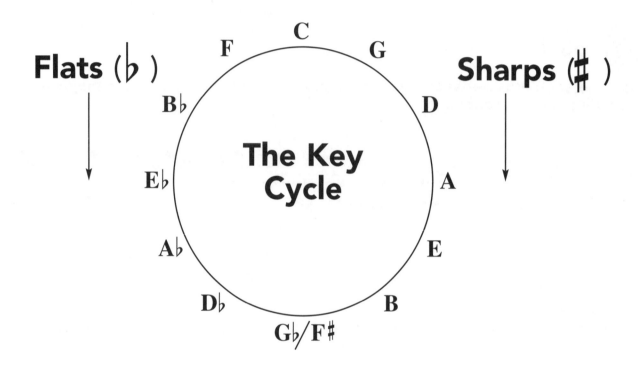

Think of the key cycle like a clock. Just as there are 12 points on the clock, there are also 12 keys. **C** is at the top and contains no sharps or flats. Moving around clockwise you will find the next key is **G**, which contains one sharp (**F♯**). The next key is **D**, which contains two sharps (**F♯** and **C♯**). Progressing further through the sharp keys each key contains an extra sharp, with the new sharp being the 7th note of the new key, and the others being any which were contained in the previous key. Therefore the key of A would automatically contain **F♯** and **C♯** which were in the key of D, plus **G♯** which is the 7th note of the A major scale. When you get to **F♯** (at 6 o'clock), the new sharp is called **E♯** which is enharmonically the same as **F**. Remember that **enharmonic** means two different ways of writing the same note. Another example of enharmonic spelling would be **F♯** and **G♭**. This means that **G♭** could become the name of the key of **F♯**. The key of **F♯** contains six sharps, while the key of **G♭** contains six flats—all of which are exactly the same notes.

If you start at **C** again at the top of the cycle and go anti-clockwise you will progress through the flat keys. The key of **F** contains one flat (**B♭**), which then becomes the name of the next key around the cycle. In flat keys, the new flat is always the 4th degree of the new key. Continuing around the cycle, the key of **B♭** contains two flats (**B♭** and **E♭**) and so on. **Practice playing all the notes around the cycle both clockwise and anticlockwise.** Once you can do this, play a **major scale** starting on each note of the cycle. In Jazz, there is a lot of movement around the cycle, so the more familiar you are with it, the better.

LESSON FIFTEEN

INTERVALS

An **interval** is the distance between two musical notes. Intervals are measured in numbers, and are calculated by counting the number of letter names (**A B C D E F G A**) between and including the notes being measured. Within an octave, intervals are: **Unison** (two notes of the same pitch played or sung together or consecutively), **2nd**, **3rd**, **4th**, **5th**, **6th**, **7th** and **Octave** (two notes an octave apart). Thus **A** to **B** is a **2nd** interval, as is B to C, C to D etc. **A** to **C** is a **3rd** interval, **A** to **D** is a **4th**, **A** to **E** is a **5th**, **A** to **F** is a **6th**, **A** to **G** is a **7th** and **A** to the next **A** is an **octave**.

Intervals may be **melodic** (two notes played consecutively) or **harmonic** (two notes played at the same time). Hence two people singing at the same time are said to be singing in harmony.

INTERVAL QUALITIES

Different intervals have different qualities, as shown below:

Quality	Can be applied to
Perfect	Unisons, 4ths, 5ths and Octaves
Major	2nds, 3rds, 6ths and 7ths
Minor	2nds, 3rds, 6ths and 7ths
Augmented	All intervals
Diminished	All intervals

These intervals can be best explained with the aid of a chromatic scale. If you look at the one below, it is easy to see that since **intervals are measured in semitones**, they may begin or end on a sharp or flat rather than a natural note.

A A#/Bb B C C#/Db D D#/Eb E F F#/Gb G G#/Ab A

Perfect intervals are **4ths**, **5ths** and **octaves**. If you **widen** a perfect interval by a semitone it becomes **augmented** (added to). E.g. if you add a semitone to the perfect 4th interval **C** to **F**, it becomes the **augmented 4th interval C** to **F#**. Notice that the letter name remains the same—it is not referred to as C to Gb.

If you narrow a perfect interval by a semitone they become **diminished** (lessened). E.g. if you lessen the perfect 5th interval **D** to **A** by a semitone, it becomes the **diminished 5th interval D to Ab**. Again, the letter name remains the same—it is not referred to as D to G#.

Major intervals (2nds, 3rds, 6ths and 7ths) become minor if narrowed by a semitone and **minor** intervals become major if widened by a semitone. A **diminished** interval can be created by narrowing a perfect or minor interval by a semitone. An **augmented** interval can be created by widening a perfect or major interval by a semitone.

INTERVAL DISTANCES

In summary, here is a list of the distances of all common intervals up to an octave measured in semitones. Each new interval is one semitone wider apart than the previous one. Notice that the interval of an octave is exactly twelve semitones. This is because there are twelve different notes in the chromatic scale. Notice also that the interval which has a distance of six semitones can be called either an augmented 4th or a perfect 5th. This interval is also often called a **tritone** (6 semitones = 3 tones).

Minor 2nd - One semitone

Major 2nd - Two semitones

Minor 3rd - Three semitones

Major 3rd - Four semitones

Perfect 4th - Five semitones

Augmented 4th or Diminished 5th - Six semitones

Perfect 5th - Seven semitones

Minor 6th - Eight semitones

Major 6th - Nine semitones

Minor 7th - Ten semitones

Major 7th - Eleven semitones

Perfect Octave - Twelve semitones

The following example demonstrates all of the common intervals ascending within one octave starting and ending on the note C.

54

minor 2nd   major 2nd   minor 3rd

perfect 4th   diminished 5th   perfect 5th   minor 6th

major 6th   minor 7th   major 7th   perfect octave

FINDING INTERVALS ON THE FRETBOARD

As well as understanding how intervals work, you need to be able to instantly play them on your instrument either ascending, descending, or harmonically from any given note. The diagrams below show the most common ways of playing intervals on the guitar. Learn them one at a time and listen carefully to the sound of each interval as you play it.

Minor 2nd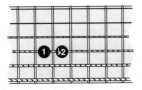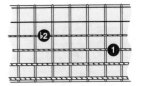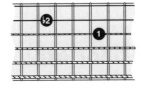

Major 2nd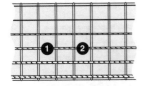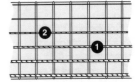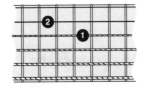

Minor 3rd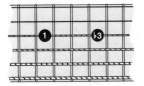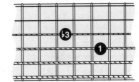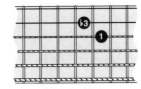

Major 3rd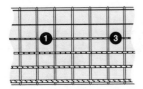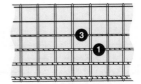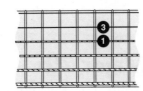

Perfect 4th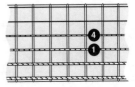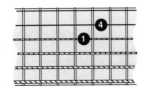

Tritone -Aug 4th or Dim 5th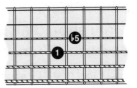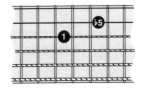

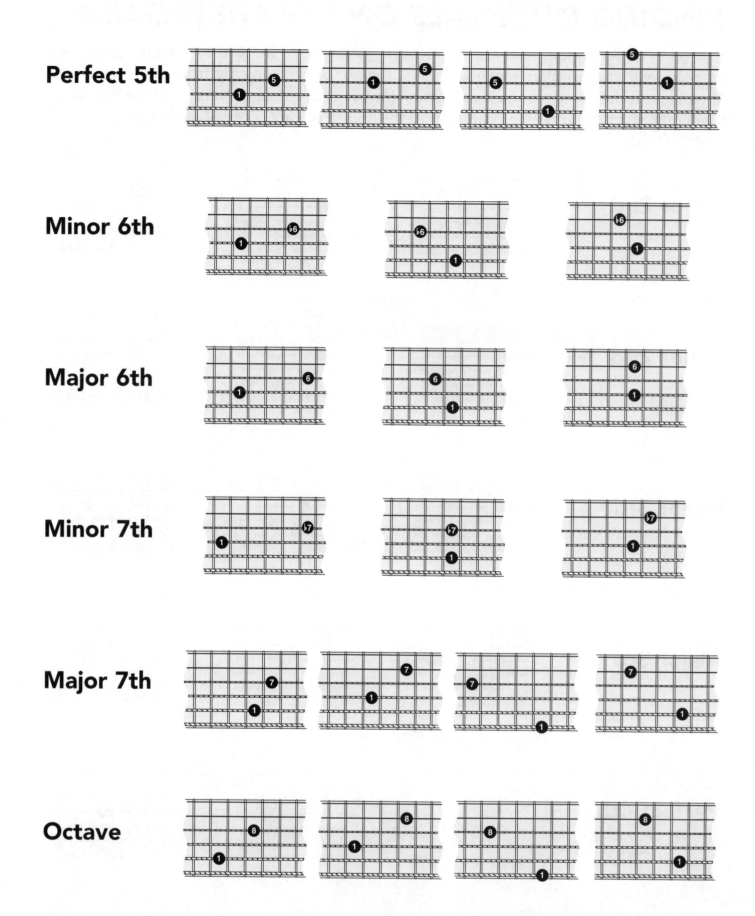

Perfect 5th

Minor 6th

Major 6th

Minor 7th

Major 7th

Octave

These diagrams show the most common ways of playing intervals on the guitar, but they are not the only patterns. You should also work on playing every possible interval on one string. This is fairly easy because all you have to do is work out how many frets apart the interval is: e.g. a perfect 4th is five frets apart, a minor 6th is eight frets apart, etc.

LESSON SIXTEEN

IDENTIFYING INTERVALS BY EAR

Since **all melodies are made up of a series of intervals**, it is essential to learn to identify intervals by ear and be able to reproduce them at will both with your voice and on your instrument. If you can sing something accurately, it means you are hearing it accurately. Here are some ways of developing your ability to identify and reproduce intervals. The example given in the first two exercises is a minor 3rd, but it is essential to go through these processes with **all** intervals.

1. Choose an interval you wish to work on (e.g. minor 3rds). Play a starting note (e.g. C) and sing it. Then sing a minor 3rd up from that note (E♭). Hold the note with your voice while you test its accuracy on your instrument. Then choose another starting note and repeat the process. Keep doing this until you are accurate every time. The next step is to sing the interval (in this case a minor 3rd) downwards from your starting note. Again, do this repeatedly until you are accurate every time.

2. Sing the same interval consecutively upwards and then downwards several times. E.g. start on C and sing a minor 3rd up from it (E♭). Then sing a minor 3rd up from E♭ (G♭). Then another minor third up from G♭ (B♭♭ - which is enharmonically the same as A). Then up another minor 3rd (C an octave higher than the starting note). Once you can do this, reverse the process (Start on C and sing a minor 3rd down to A, then another minor 3rd down and then another, etc).

3. Play and sing a starting note (e.g. C) and then think of it as the first degree of the chromatic scale - sing "one". Now sing the flattened second degree of the scale - sing "flat two". This note is a minor 2nd up from your C note (a D♭ note). Then sing the C again ("one"). Then sing the second degree of the scale (a D note - sing "two"). Next, sing your C Note again ("one"). Continue in this manner all the way up the chromatic scale until you reach C an octave above. The entire sequence goes: 1, ♭2, 1, 2, 1, ♭3, 1, 3, 1, 4, 1, ♭5, 1, 5, 1, ♭6, 1, 6, 1, ♭7, 1, 7, 1, 8, 1. As with the previous exercises, once you can do this accurately (check your pitches on your instrument), reverse the process and sing downwards from the top of the scale, working your way down the chromatic scale again. The downward sequence goes 1(8), 7, 1, ♭7, 1, 6, 1, ♭6, 1, 5, 1, ♭5, 1, 4, 1, 3, 1, ♭3, 1, 2, 1, ♭2, 1, 1, 1(8).

4. As well as hearing intervals melodically (one note at a time), it is important to be able to hear them harmonically (two notes played together). A good way to develop this is to have a friend play random harmonic intervals on either guitar or keyboard while you identify them. Keep your back to the instrument while you do this, so that you cannot identify the intervals by sight.

It is important to work at these things regularly until they become easy. Don't get frustrated if you can't hear intervals accurately at first. Most people have trouble with this. If you work at it for several months, you will see a dramatic improvement in your musical hearing, and will be able to improvise much more freely as well as being able to work out parts off CDs more easily.

INTERVALS IN SEQUENCES

Once you have a basic understanding of how intervals work, it is a good idea to practice playing scales in interval sequences. As mentioned earlier, a **sequence** is a repetitive pattern in which the rhythm remains the same while the pitches are repeated higher or lower, usually within a specific scale or mode. The following examples demonstrate intervals played through various major scales. Because of the pattern of tones and semitones within the major scale, you will find that various types of intervals occur rather than all being the one type. E.g. example 57 shows the **C** major scale played ascending and descending in **2nds**. All of the intervals are 2nds but some of them are major 2nds (e.g. C to D and D to E) and some are minor 2nds (e.g. E to F and B to C).

55   (2nds)

56   (3rds)

Here is the **F** major scale played in 3rds. Once again, some are major and some are minor.

57   (4ths)

This example shows the **A** major scale played in **4ths**. All of the intervals here are perfect 4ths except for D to G♯ which is an augmented 4th.

58   (5ths)

Here is the **B♭** major scale played in **5ths**. All of the intervals are perfect 5ths except for A to E♭ which is a diminished 5th.

59 (6ths)

This one demonstrates the **G** major scale played in **6ths**. Again, some are major and some are minor. As the intervals get larger, these examples will probably become more difficult to play. Take them slowly at first but stick with it, as a good knowledge of intervals is essential for improvising.

60 (7ths)

This example shows the **A♭** major scale played in **7ths**. As with previous interval studies you will find that some of the 7ths here are major and some are minor.

61 (Octaves)

It is also important to be able to play your scales in octaves. Using octaves is a common Jazz guitar technique made popular by **Wes Montgomery**. Playing in octaves requires quite a bit of movement along the fretboard. The following example demonstrates the **E** major scale played in **octaves**.

62

As well as learning your scales with all the intervals, it is important to practice improvising and concentrating on a particular interval. The following example makes extensive use of **4ths**.

Am⁷

63 Blue Note Blues

Here is a **12 bar Blues** solo in the key of **B♭** which makes use of many different intervals. Go through it and analyze the intervals and also the scale degrees against a **B♭ chromatic scale**. Notice the use of both major and minor 3rd degrees, as well as the flattened 5th and 7th degrees of the scale. The ♭3, ♭5 and ♭7 are known as **blue notes** and are particularly common in Blues. Blues playing is discussed in detail in *Progressive Jazz Lead Guitar Technique*, which follows on from this book.

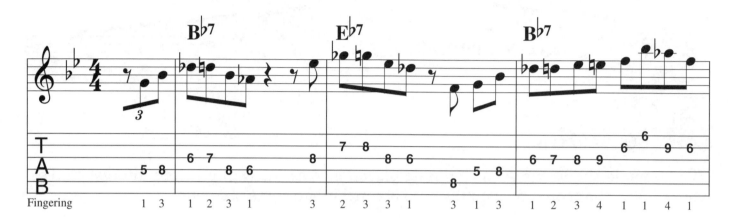

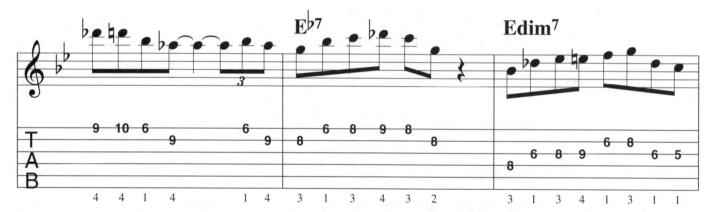

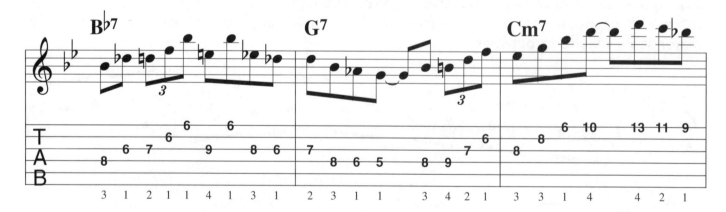

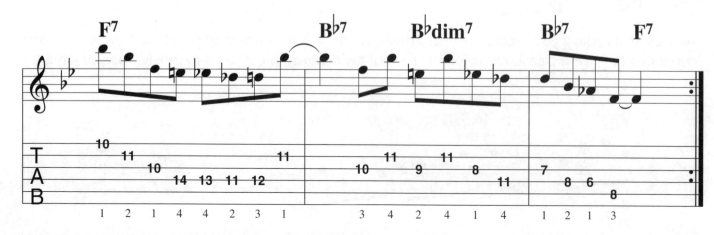

SECTION 3

Understanding Chord Progressions, Arpeggios and Modes

LESSON SEVENTEEN

UNDERSTANDING CHORDS

A **chord** is a group of three or more notes played simultaneously. Different types of chords can be formed by using different combinations of notes. The most basic type of chord contains three different notes and is called a **triad**. The most common triads are **major chords**. All major chords contain three notes taken from the major scale of the same letter name. These three notes are the **1** (first), **3** (third) and **5** (fifth) degrees of the major scale, so the **chord formula** for the major chord is:

Chord Symbol	**1 3 5**	*Notes in Chord*
C	**The C Major Chord**	C E G 1 3 5

The C major chord is constructed from the C major scale. Using the above chord formula on the C major scale below, it can be seen that the C major chord contains the notes **C**, **E** and **G**.

C Major Scale

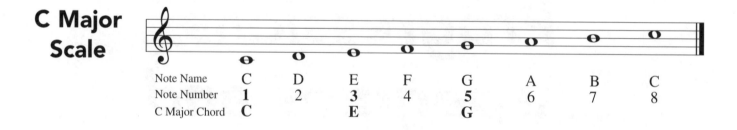

Note Name	C	D	E	F	G	A	B	C
Note Number	**1**	2	**3**	4	**5**	6	7	8
C Major Chord	**C**		**E**		**G**			

Once you have the correct notes for a C chord they can be arranged in any order. As long as the notes are still C, E and G, you still have a C chord. E.g. a C chord could be played C E G, or E G C, or G C E, or even G E C. These various arrangements of the notes within a chord are called **inversions**. It is also possible to **double** notes within a chord. E.g. the diagram below shows a common way of playing a C major chord on the guitar. It contains two C notes and two E notes. It is still a C major chord because it only contains notes called C, E and G. Doubling notes is common when playing chords on the guitar.

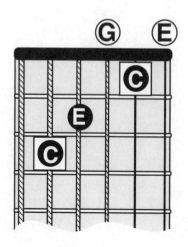

Arpeggios

Up to this point, everything you have learnt has been based on the use of scales. There are also other important groupings of notes called **arpeggios**. An arpeggio is a chord played one note at a time. The value of arpeggios is that they enable you to play lines which fit chord progressions perfectly, since every note of an arpeggio is a note of the accompanying chord. Written below is a **C major arpeggio** which consists of the notes **C**, **E** and **G**. These are the **root**, **third** and **fifth** of a **C major chord**.

64.0

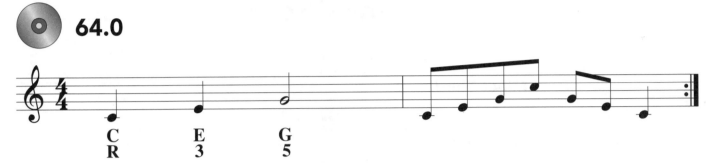

Here is an **F major arpeggio** which consists of the notes **F**, **A** and **C**. These are the root, third and fifth of an **F major chord**.

64.1

Like scales, it is important to be able to play arpeggios in every key. The following example demonstrates major arpeggios played around the key cycle. Play them all in the first position and then move them through all five forms. Name each arpeggio as you play.

64.2

CHORD CONSTRUCTION - TRIADS

Chords are usually made up of combinations of major and minor third intervals. As mentioned previously, the simplest chords are made up of three notes and are called **triads**. There are **four** basic types of triads: **major**, **minor**, **augmented** and **diminished**. Examples of each of these are shown below along with the formula for each one.

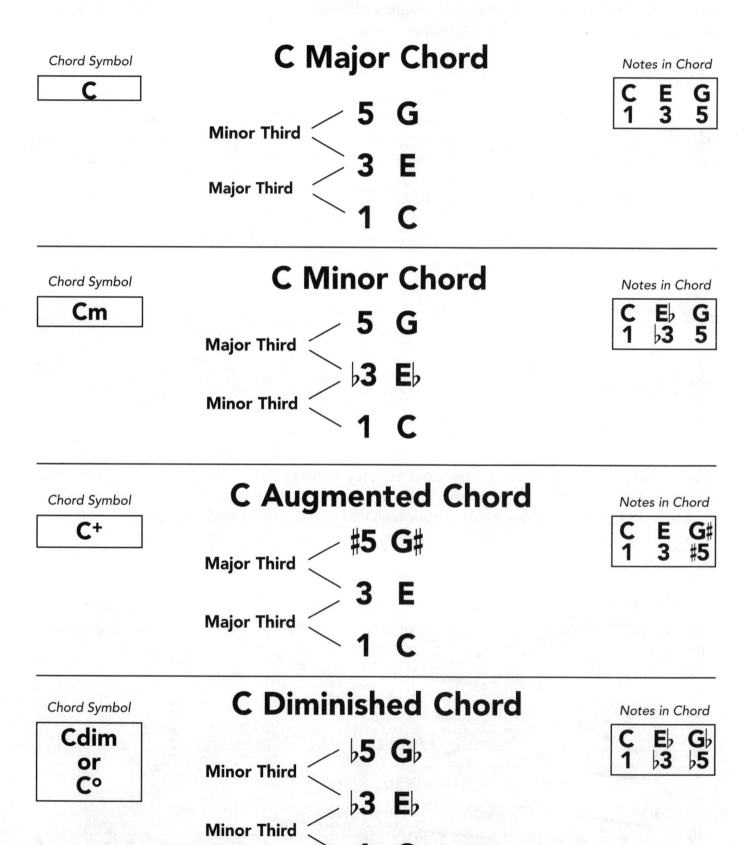

C Major Chord

Chord Symbol

C

Minor Third — 5 G
Major Third — 3 E
— 1 C

Notes in Chord

C E G
1 3 5

C Minor Chord

Chord Symbol

Cm

Major Third — 5 G
Minor Third — ♭3 E♭
— 1 C

Notes in Chord

C E♭ G
1 ♭3 5

C Augmented Chord

Chord Symbol

C+

Major Third — ♯5 G♯
Major Third — 3 E
— 1 C

Notes in Chord

C E G♯
1 3 ♯5

C Diminished Chord

Chord Symbol

Cdim
or
C°

Minor Third — ♭5 G♭
Minor Third — ♭3 E♭
— 1 C

Notes in Chord

C E♭ G♭
1 ♭3 ♭5

For every type of chord there is a corresponding arpeggio. This means there are major, minor, augmented, diminished, dominant seventh and minor seventh arpeggios among others. Shown below is a **C minor arpeggio** which consists of the notes **C**, **E♭** and **G** which are the **root**, **flattened third** and **fifth** of a **C minor chord**.

 65.0

 65.1

This is a **G minor arpeggio** which consists of the notes **G**, **B♭** and **D**. These are the root, third and fifth of a **G minor chord**.

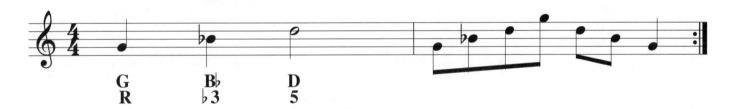

 65.2

Here are all the minor arpeggios between **C minor** and **B minor** played chromatically ascending. Try playing them chromatically descending as well. Once again, you will need to know how to play these arpeggios in all possible positions on the fretboard.

LESSON EIGHTEEN

ARPEGGIOS AND CHORD PROGRESSIONS

Once you have a basic understanding of arpeggios, it is important to practice them over chord progressions as well as around the cycle or chromatically. The following example shows a **12 bar Blues** progression in the key of **C minor** played entirely with arpeggios. Listen to the recording to hear how all the notes fit the progression perfectly. This must be so, because the notes of the arpeggios are identical to the notes of the chords used in the accompaniment. Being able to make your lines fit any given chord progression is one of the most important elements of Jazz playing. Using arpeggios is one of the most common ways of achieving this.

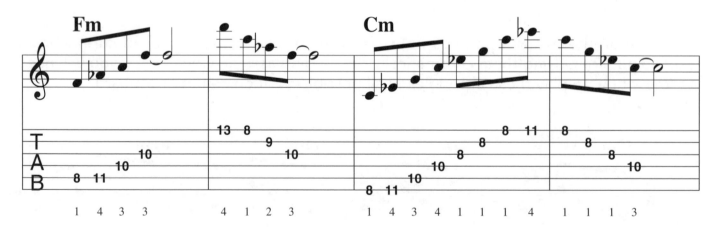

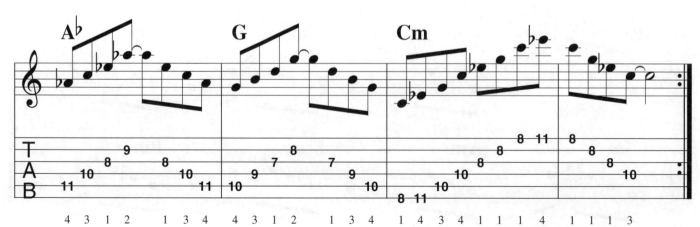

IMPROVISING WITH ARPEGGIOS

Once you are comfortable playing through a chord progression using arpeggios, try improvising more freely with the notes instead of simply running up and down the arpeggios (although this **is** an essential first step). If you have trouble, use some set rhythms until it becomes easier. The following example uses the same 12 bar Blues progression in **C minor**, but the lines are much freer both melodically and rhythmically. Notice that when a chord change occurs the line moves to the nearest note of the arpeggio of the new chord rather than starting on the root note of each new chord. This results in a much smoother and more logical melodic line.

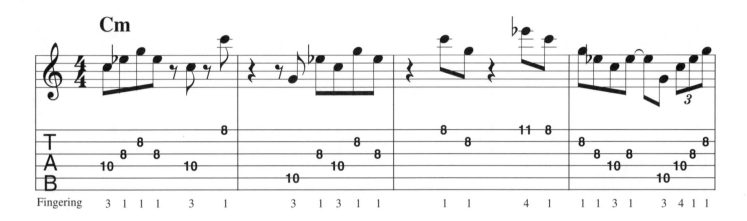

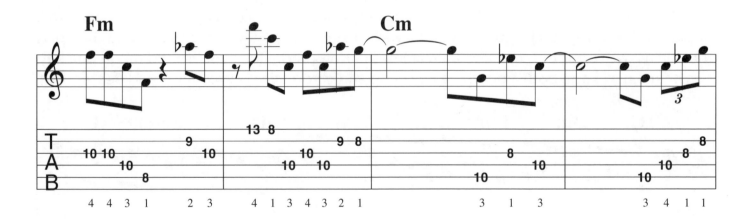

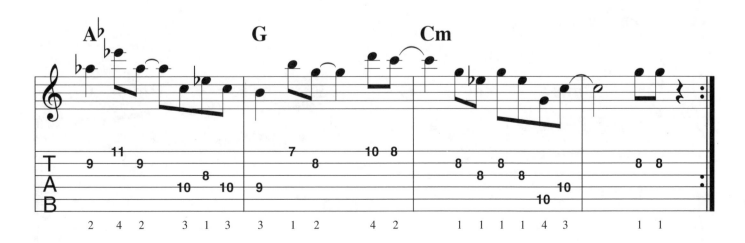

LESSON NINETEEN

SCALE TONE CHORDS

In any key it is possible to build chords on each degree of the scale. This means that for every major scale there are **seven** possible chords which can be used for creating and harmonizing melodies. These seven chords are called **scale tone chords**. It is common practice to describe all the chords within a key with **roman numerals** as shown in the example below which demonstrates the seven scale tone triads in the key of **C major**.

 68

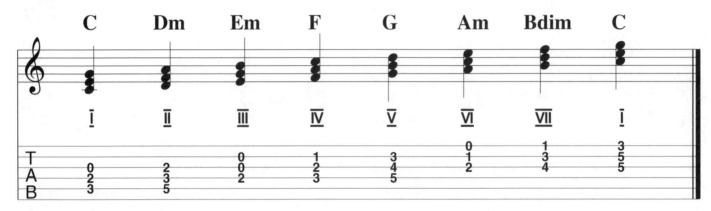

 69

Here are the seven scale tone triads in **C** major played as arpeggios. The ascending pattern in bars 1 to 4 begins on the **root** of each new chord, while the descending pattern in bars 5 to 8 begins on the **5th** of each new chord. As always, learn them in the first position and then play them in all five forms of the major scale along the fretboard. Once you can do this in one key, play them in all keys; both around the key cycle and chromatically ascending and descending.

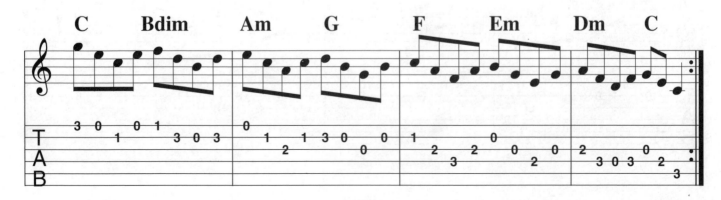

MAJOR KEY TRIAD PATTERN

If you go through and analyse all of the scale tone chords in the key of C major you come up with the following pattern:

I̲	Major	(C Major)
I̲I̲	Minor	(D Minor)
I̲I̲I̲	Minor	(E Minor)
I̲V̲	Major	(F Major)
V̲	Major	(G Major)
V̲I̲	Minor	(A Minor)
V̲I̲I̲	Diminished	(B Diminished)

This pattern remains the same regardless of the key. This means that if you look at the scale tone triads in **any major key**, Chord I̲ is **always** major, chord I̲I̲ is always minor, chord I̲I̲I̲ is always minor, etc. The only thing that changes from one key to the next is the letter names of the chords. This can be demonstrated by looking at the scale tone triads for the key of G major which are shown below.

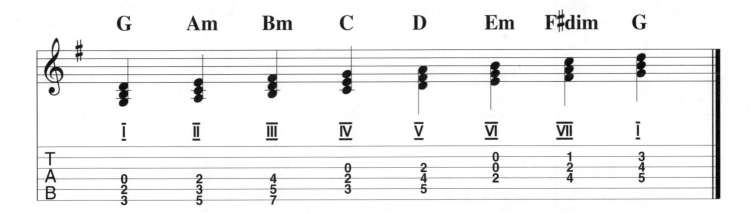

By simply following the roman numerals and remembering which chords are major, minor, etc, it is easy to transpose chords from one key to another. Here is a chord progression shown in both **C** major and **G** major, along with the roman numerals for each chord.

SCALE TONE CHORDS IN ALL KEYS

The chart below lists the scale tone chords in all major keys. However, to become thoroughly familiar with scale tone chords, you will need to write out all 13 major scales and build chords on each of them, being careful to observe the correct sharps or flats for each key. Once you know the notes in each chord, you can use any fingering for the chord that sounds good to you.

Summary of Scale Tone Chords

Scale Note:	Ī	ĪĪ	ĪĪĪ	ĪV	V̄	V̄Ī	V̄ĪĪ	V̄ĪĪĪ (Ī)
Chord Constructed:	major	minor	minor	major	major	minor	dim	major
C Scale	C	Dm	Em	F	G	Am	B°	C
G Scale	G	Am	Bm	C	D	Em	F#°	G
D Scale	D	Em	F#m	G	A	Bm	C#°	D
A Scale	A	Bm	C#m	D	E	F#m	G#°	A
E Scale	E	F#m	G#m	A	B	C#m	D#°	E
B Scale	B	C#m	D#m	E	F#	G#m	A#°	B
F# Scale	F#	G#m	A#m	B	C#	D#m	E#° (F°)	F#
F Scale	F	Gm	Am	Bb	C	Dm	E°	F
Bb Scale	Bb	Cm	Dm	Eb	F	Gm	A°	Bb
Eb Scale	Eb	Fm	Gm	Ab	Bb	Cm	D°	Eb
Ab Scale	Ab	Bbm	Cm	Db	Eb	Fm	G°	Ab
Db Scale	Db	Ebm	Fm	Gb	Ab	Bbm	C°	Db
Gb Scale	Gb	Abm(G#m)	Bbm	Cb (B)	Db	Ebm	F°	Gb

COMMON PROGRESSIONS

One of the best ways to become familiar with chords in all keys is to take a simple progression and transpose it to all of the keys. This may be slow at first, but the more you do it, the easier it gets. Here are some common progressions to learn and transpose. Play through each progression as both chords and arpeggios until you are totally familiar with them, as these progressions occur frequently in Jazz standards.

Ī ĪV V̄ Ī

Ī V̄Ī ĪV V̄

ĪĪ V̄ Ī

Ī V̄Ī ĪĪ V̄

Ī ĪV V̄ĪĪ ĪĪĪ V̄Ī ĪĪ V̄

LESSON TWENTY

SEVENTH CHORDS

By adding more notes on top of the basic triads, it is possible to create many other types of chords. The most common types of chords used in Jazz are **seventh chords**. Various types of seventh chords are created by adding another note either a major or minor third above the basic triad. The formulas for the **five basic types** of seventh chords are shown below.

Major Seventh
Chord Formula

Chord Symbol

CMaj7

1   3   5   7

Notes in Chord

C	E	G	B
1	3	5	7

Dominant Seventh
Chord Formula

Chord Symbol

C7

1   3   5   ♭7

Notes in Chord

C	E	G	B♭
1	3	5	♭7

Minor Seventh
Chord Formula

Chord Symbol

Cm7

1   ♭3   5   ♭7

Notes in Chord

C	E♭	G	B♭
1	♭3	5	♭7

Minor Seven Flat Five
Chord Formula

Chord Symbol

Cm7♭5

1   ♭3   ♭5   ♭7

Notes in Chord

C	E♭	G♭	B♭
1	♭3	♭5	♭7

The final type of seventh chord is the diminished seventh. This chord is unusual in that it contains a **double flattened 7th** degree (♭♭7). This note is actually the same as the 6th degree (A) but it is technically called **B♭♭7** because the interval has to be some kind of seventh rather than a sixth because the chord is a type of **seventh** chord.

Diminished Seventh
Chord Formula

Chord Symbol

C°7♭

1   ♭3   ♭5   ♭♭7

Notes in Chord

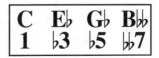

C	E♭	G♭	B♭♭
1	♭3	♭5	♭♭7

LEARNING TO PLAY SEVENTH CHORDS

To become thoroughly familiar with the various 7th chord types in every key, you will need to write them out starting on all twelve notes of the chromatic scale (using both sharps and flats). Work on one type of 7th chord at a time until you know them all. It is also important to practice them on your instrument as arpeggios around the key cycle and chromatically up and down.

MAJOR SEVENTHS

A **major seventh** chord is created by adding a **major 3rd** on top of a **major triad**. As with triads, there are many different ways of playing major 7th arpeggios on the guitar fretboard. Some of these are shown in the following diagrams.

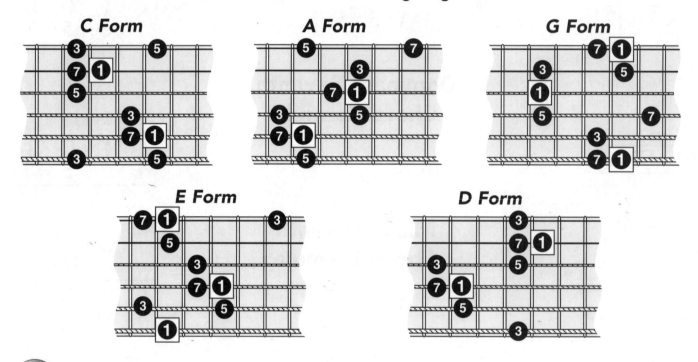

70   **Major 7ths Around the Cycle**

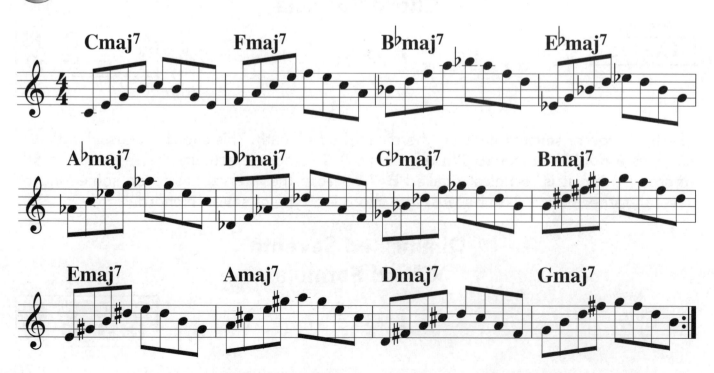

Once you start to feel comfortable with the various fingerings for major 7th arpeggios, try improvising with them and moving between the various forms as shown in the example below.

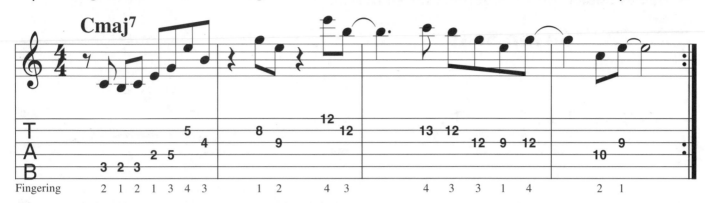

DOMINANT SEVENTHS

A **dominant seventh** chord (often just called a **7th** chord – **C7**, **B♭7**, etc) is created by adding a **minor 3rd** on top of a **major triad**. The diagrams below show some common fretboard patterns for playing dominant 7th arpeggios. However, these are not the only ways to play 7th chords. As with everything you learn, you should constantly experiment to find other ways to play each new chord type.

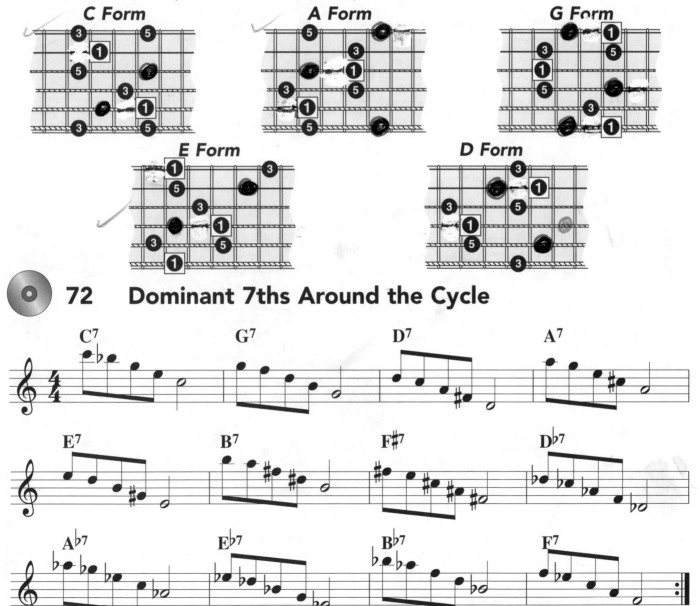

72   Dominant 7ths Around the Cycle

78

Dominant 7th arpeggios are commonly used when playing over Blues progressions. Run through the basic progression first using arpeggios starting on the root note and then try improvising with the notes of the arpeggios as shown in the following example. Learn this solo in the key of **B♭**, analyze all the chord tones and then transpose it to all other keys, as well as finding other fingerings for all the lines.

73   Seven Seas

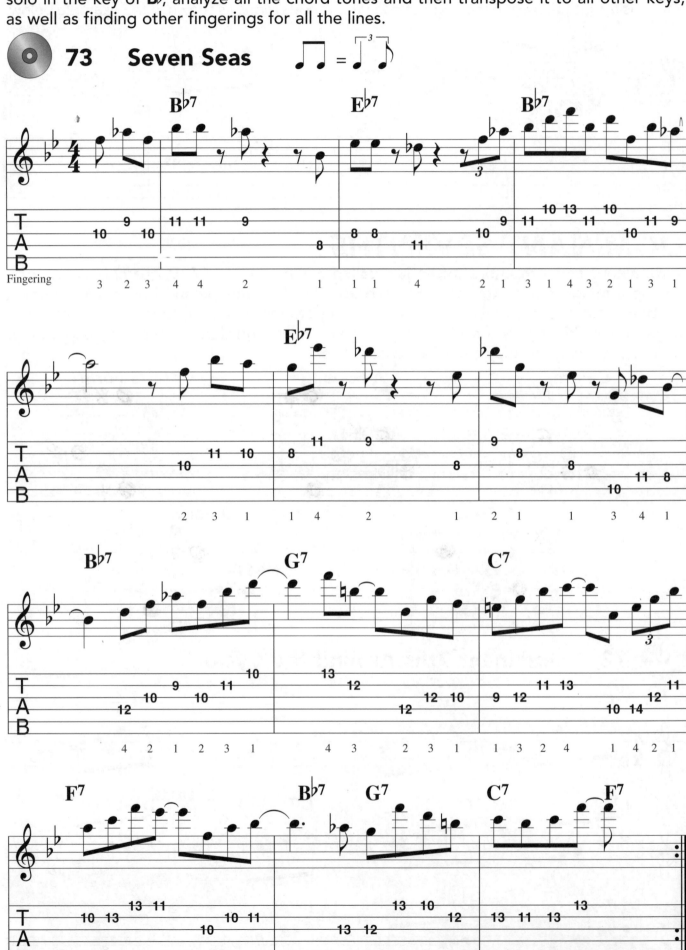

MINOR SEVENTHS

A **minor seventh** chord is created by adding a **minor 3rd** on top of a **minor triad**. The diagrams below show some common fretboard patterns for playing minor7th arpeggios. As with previous chord types, look for other ways of playing them as well.

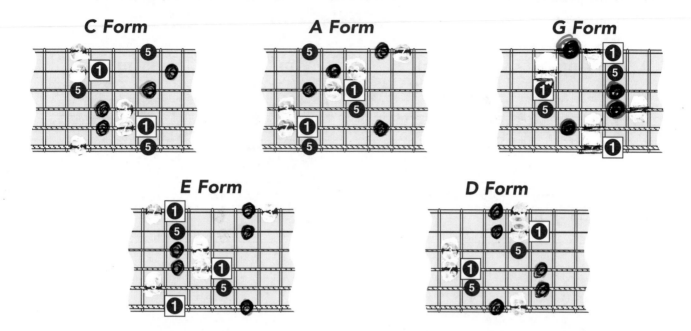

PRACTICING SCALES AND ARPEGGIOS

When you play Jazz tunes, the root movement of the chord progression may consist of **any** interval between one chord and the next. To be prepared for this, it is a good idea to practice all your scales and arpeggios ascending and descending with all possible intervals. The following example demonstrates **minor 7th** arpeggios **descending in major 2nd intervals**. There are **two sets of intervals** here – one set descending from **C** and the other descending from **B**. Try this practice method with other intervals: e.g. minor and major 3rds.

 74   **Minor 7ths Descending in Major 2nds**

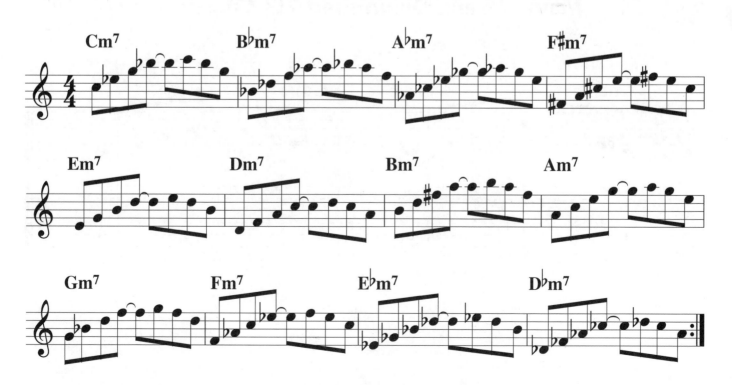

Once you start to feel comfortable with the various fingerings for minor 7th arpeggios, remember to practice improvising with them in all five forms over chord progressions.

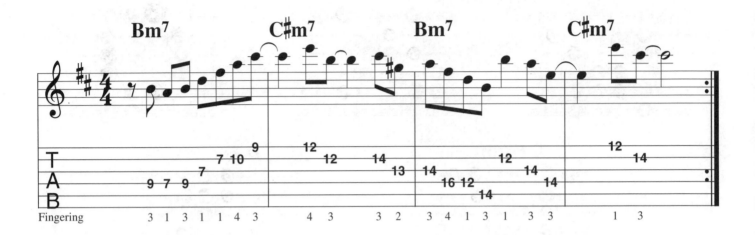

MINOR 7 FLAT FIVE AND DIMINISHED 7THS

The final two types of seventh chords are the Minor 7 flat 5 (**m7♭5**) and the diminished 7th (**°7** or **dim7**). These chords are dealt with in detail in *Progressive Jazz Lead Guitar Technique*. Shown below are arpeggios of both these chord types. Memorize the formula for each one (shown on page 77) and the sound as well, and then work out other fingerings for the arpeggios. Experiment with them over their respective chords and then find some songs which use these chords to practice improvising with them.

 76   Minor 7♭5 and Diminished 7th Chords

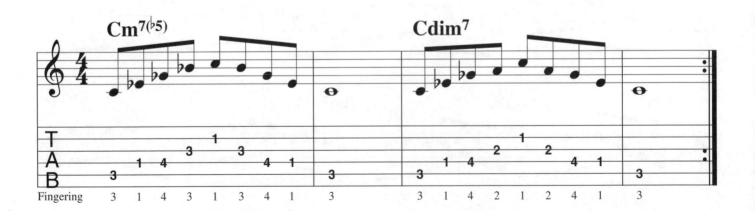

LESSON TWENTY ONE

SCALE TONE 7TH CHORDS

By applying the formulas for seventh chords to the C major scale, the following series of chords is created. These are called **scale tone seventh chords**. If you analyze the notes of these scale tone 7th chords, you will notice that they are all based on the C major scale tone triads and each one has another 3rd interval added above it.

Cmaj7	Dm7	Em7	Fmaj7	G7	Am7	Bm7♭5
Ī	IĪ	IIĪ	IV̄	V̄	Vī	VIĪ

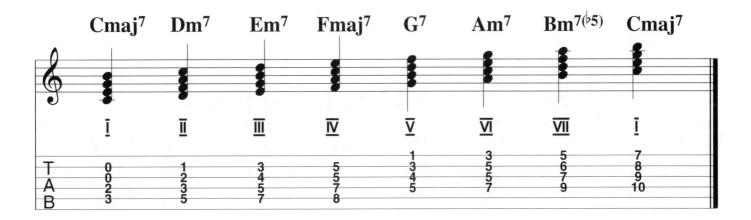

It is essential to be able to play these scale tone 7th chords as arpeggios in all five forms on the fretboard, and in all twelve keys. Here is an example in C major. Learn it from memory in the open position and then work out the other fingerings as well as transposing it to all the other keys.

 77

SCALE TONE 7TH PATTERN

Like triads, the pattern of scale tone 7th chord types remains the same for every key. The pattern is summarized below. The minor 7 flat 5 chord is also sometimes called a half diminished chord (ø7).

I	II	III	IV	V	VI	VII	VIII
major7	m7	m7	maj7	7	m7	m7♭5 or (ø7)	maj7

The following chart shows scale tone 7th chords in all keys. If you intend to play Jazz, or any kind of Fusion music, it is essential to memorize all these chords. Work through each key and then take a simple progression and play it in every key. Then try a longer progression, then a song containing the various 7th chord types. The more you do this, the easier it gets.

Scale Tone 7ths in all Keys

I	II	III	IV	V	VI	VII	VIII
Major7	**Minor7**	**Minor7**	**Major7**	**7**	**Minor7**	**Minor7♭5**	**Major7**
Cmaj7	Dm7	Em7	Fmaj7	G7	Am7	Bm7♭5	Cmaj7
Gmaj7	Am7	Bm7	Cmaj7	D7	Em7	F♯m7♭5	Gmaj7
Dmaj7	Em7	F♯m7	Gmaj7	A7	Bm7	C♯m7♭5	Dmaj7
Amaj7	Bm7	C♯m7	Dmaj7	E7	F♯m7	G♯m7♭5	Amaj7
Emaj7	F♯m7	G♯m7	Amaj7	B7	C♯m7	D♯m7♭5	Emaj7
Bmaj7	C♯m7	D♯m7	Emaj7	F♯7	G♯m7	A♯m7♭5	Bmaj7
F♯maj7	G♯m7	A♯m7	Bmaj7	C♯7	D♯m7	E♯(F)m7♭5	F♯maj7
Fmaj7	Gm7	Am7	B♭maj7	C7	Dm7	Em7♭5	Fmaj7
B♭maj7	Cm7	Dm7	E♭maj7	F7	Gm7	Am7♭5	B♭maj7
E♭maj7	Fm7	Gm7	A♭maj7	B♭7	Cm7	Dm7♭5	E♭maj7
A♭maj7	B♭m7	Cm7	D♭maj7	E♭7	Fm7	Gm7♭5	A♭maj7
D♭maj7	E♭m7	Fm7	G♭maj7	A♭7	B♭m7	Cm7♭5	D♭maj7
G♭maj7	A♭m7	B♭m7	C♭(B) maj7	D♭7	E♭m7	Fm7♭5	G♭maj7

LESSON TWENTY TWO

THE II V I PROGRESSION

Once you know how to play scale tone 7th chords, the next step is using them to improvise over chord progressions within a key. One of the most common progressions used in Jazz is the II V I progression. As the name implies, this progression begins on the second chord in the key (IIm7), progresses to the fifth (V7) and then progresses to the chord which the key is named from (Imaj7). A good way to become familiar with this (or any) progression is to record yourself playing the chords, or use a play-along CD and play the arpeggios of the chords over the backing. The example below shows this procedure in the key of **C**. Learn it in this key and then transpose it to all the other keys.

Once you are comfortable running through the arpeggios against the chords, try improvising with the arpeggios as shown here. Once again, learn this example and then transpose it to all keys. As stated earlier, this process is essential if you wish to become a good Jazz player. You should now be doing it as a matter of course with everything you learn.

It is also common for II V I progressions to occur over two bars rather than four as shown below. As with the four bar version, practice running through the arpeggios and then improvising with them. Remember to do this in all keys.

OTHER COMMON PROGRESSIONS

After the II V I progression, the next most common major key progression is I VI II V, or VI II V I. Like the II V I progression, run through the arpeggios of these chords over a backing track of the chords (or better still, practice with another musician and take it in turns to solo or play chords) and then improvise using the arpeggios. Here is an example played over a I VI II V progression. Learn it from memory and then transpose it to all the other keys.

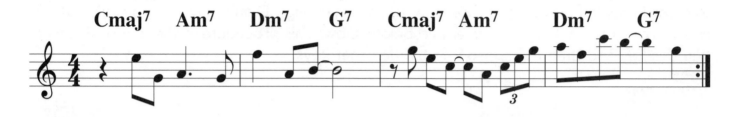

Here is a progression which covers all the chords in a major key: I IV VII III VI II V. As with previous examples, memorize both the progression and the individual notes and learn it in all keys.

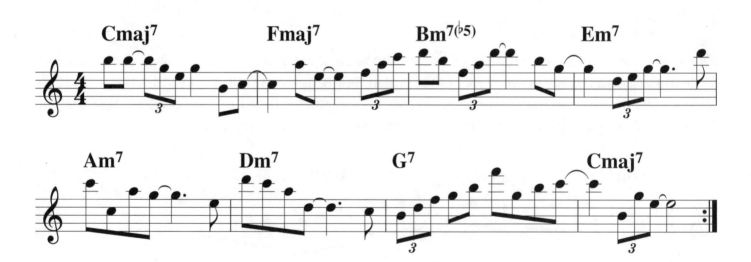

In many Jazz songs, a II V progression does not lead to chord I, but to another II V in a different Key. Here is an example.

84 Latin Satin

Here is a whole solo making use of short II V progressions moving through several different keys. Notice that the eighth notes are played straight rather than swung here. Once you can play the solo, analyze the notes against the chord symbols and then transpose it to all the other keys as well as improvising over the progression.

LESSON TWENTY THREE

MODES

As mentioned in section 1, there are **seven** different modes which can be derived from the major scale by starting on each of the seven notes of the major scale. These modes were first used in ancient Greece and have been widely used throughout history in all types of music. They are particularly useful for improvising or composing melodies over chord progressions. The names of the seven modes and their relationship to the major scale are shown below.

1. Ionian mode – The Ionian mode is another name for the major scale itself. By starting and ending on the **first** note of the major scale (**C**) you can play the Ionian mode.

C Ionian = C D E F G A B C

2. Dorian mode – The Dorian mode starts and ends on the **second** note of the major scale (in this case **D**).

D Dorian = D E F G A B C D

3. Phrygian mode – The Phrygian mode starts and ends on the **third** note of the major scale (in this case **E**).

E Phrygian = E F G A B C D E

4. Lydian mode – The Lydian mode starts and ends on the **fourth** note of the major scale (in this case **F**).

F Lydian = F G A B C D E F

5. Mixolydian mode – The Mixolydian mode starts and ends on the **fifth** note of the major scale (in this case **G**).

G Mixolydian = G A B C D E F G

6. Aeolian mode – The Aeolian mode starts and ends on the **sixth** note of the major scale (in this case **A**).

A Aeolian = A B C D E F G A

7. Locrian mode – The Locrian mode starts and ends on the **seventh** note of the major scale (in this case **B**).

B Locrian = B C D E F G A B

85

Example 86 shows the seven modes derived from the C major scale played against the seven scale tone seventh chords from the key of C major.

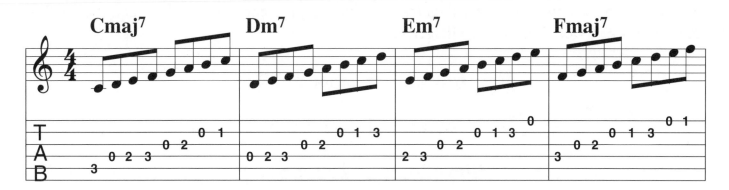

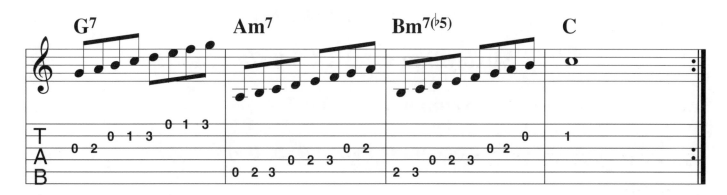

86

Because each seventh chord contains four notes of the mode it relates to, modes work extremely well over seventh chords. Listen to the sound of this line using the **D Dorian** mode over a **Dm7 chord**. Learn this line in the open position and then move it through all five forms on the fretboard. Experiment with all the modes over the various types of seventh chords from the key of C major until you can easily recognise the sound of each mode and know which chord it works best over.

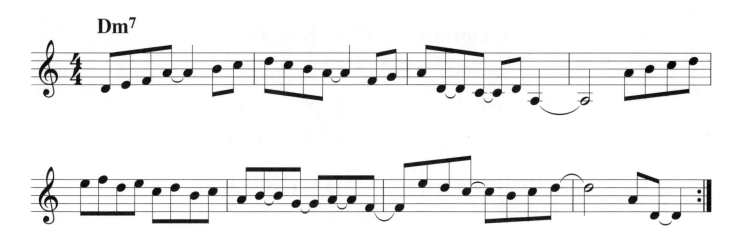

MODE FORMULAS

On the previous page you learnt all of the modes derived from the major scale. Each of these modes can be played in many different positions on the fretboard and can be played **in any key**. Just as there are twelve major keys, there are also twelve possible starting notes for each of the modes. Any note of the chromatic scale can be used as a starting note for any mode. This requires a knowledge of the formula for each mode. The scale degrees of each mode are listed below.

$$\text{Ionian} = 1\ 2\ 3\ 4\ 5\ 6\ 7$$

$$\text{Dorian} = 1\ 2\ \flat3\ 4\ 5\ 6\ \flat7$$

$$\text{Phrygian} = 1\ \flat2\ \flat3\ 4\ 5\ \flat6\ \flat7$$

$$\text{Lydian} = 1\ 2\ 3\ \sharp4\ 5\ 6\ 7$$

$$\text{Mixolydian} = 1\ 2\ 3\ 4\ 5\ 6\ \flat7$$

$$\text{Aeolian} = 1\ 2\ \flat3\ 4\ 5\ \flat6\ \flat7$$

$$\text{Locrian} = 1\ \flat2\ \flat3\ 4\ \flat5\ \flat6\ \flat7$$

To become confident using modes in your playing it will be necessary to memorize the formula for each of these modes. Don't try to memorize them all at once, take one mode at a time and learn the formula as it relates to the **sound** of the mode. Learn the fingerings for the mode and experiment with it. You should also listen to your favourite recordings and try learning some solos which use each mode. All you need to work out a mode in any key is the starting note and the formula. Here is the Dorian mode shown in four different keys.

$$\text{C Dorian} = C\ D\ E\flat\ F\ G\ A\ B\flat$$
$$1\ 2\ \flat3\ 4\ 5\ 6\ \flat7$$

$$\text{F Dorian} = F\ G\ A\flat\ B\flat\ C\ D\ E\flat$$
$$1\ 2\ \flat3\ 4\ 5\ 6\ \flat7$$

$$\text{A Dorian} = A\ B\ C\ D\ E\ F\sharp\ G$$
$$1\ 2\ \flat3\ 4\ 5\ 6\ \flat7$$

$$\text{B Dorian} = B\ C\sharp\ D\ E\ F\sharp\ G\sharp\ A$$
$$1\ 2\ \flat3\ 4\ 5\ 6\ \flat7$$

LESSON TWENTY FOUR

FINGERINGS FOR MODES

Because the seven modes can all be derived from the major scale, it can be confusing when trying to identify fingering patterns for the individual modes. Like the major scale (Ionian mode) **all** the modes can be found in five basic forms which cover the whole fretboard. In each fingering pattern it is the positions of the **root notes** (key notes or tonics) which determine the name of the form. Shown below is the **E form** of **C Ionian** which is the same as the **G form** of **D Dorian**, except for the positions of the root notes.

E Form of C Ionian

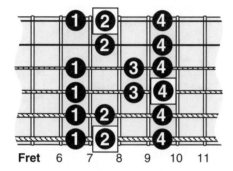

G Form of D Dorian

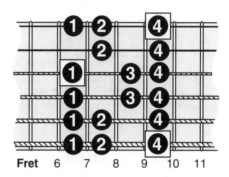

The **E form** of **C Ionian** is also the same as the **A form** of **E Phrygian**, except for the positions of the root notes. Work out the equivalent patterns for all the other modes and then find the other four forms for each one.

E Form of C Ionian

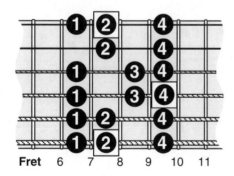

A Form of E Phrygian

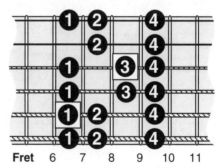

It is also important to be able to play parallel modes in the same position. Shown below is the **C Form** open position fingering for both **C Lydian** and **C Aeolian**.

C Form of C Lydian

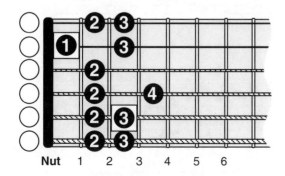

C Form of C Aeolian

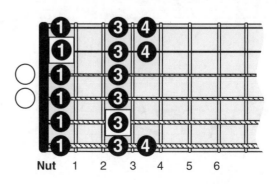

A great way to become familiar with all of the mode formulas is to play them all starting from the same note. The following example demonstrates all seven modes starting and finishing on the note C. Once you know them in this key, try starting on each different note of the chromatic scale and playing all seven modes. This will take quite some time to master, but by the time you can do it you will be much more confident in your knowledge of modes.

 87

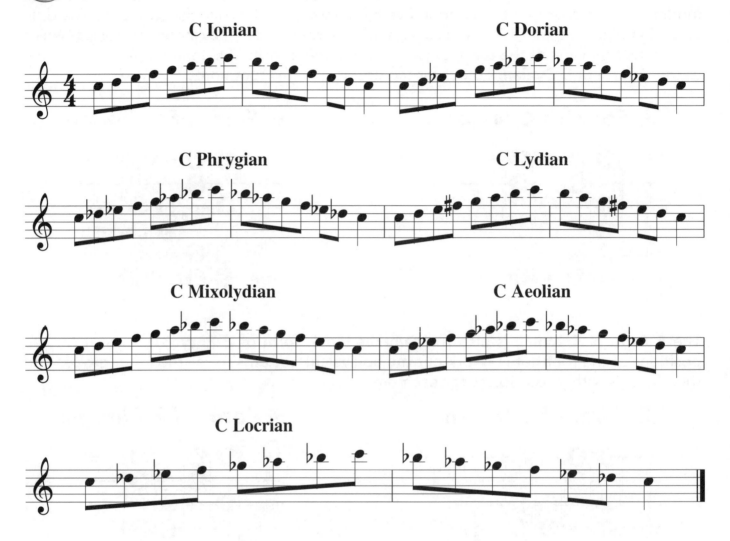

Once you know a mode in a new key, you should begin improvising with it in that key. This next example shows a line created from the E Lydian mode.

 **88**

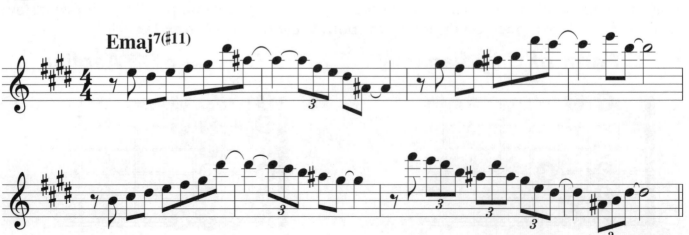

LESSON TWENTY FIVE

MODES OVER CHORD CHANGES

Whenever you begin working on a new song you wish to improvise on, it is important to analyze the chord changes (chord progression) and work out which modes will work best over them as well as the arpeggios of the chords themselves. Once you know this, run through the modes over a recorded background of the chord changes until you are comfortable with them. The following example shows a II̲ V̲ I̲ progression in the key of E♭ with the appropriate modes played over the chords.

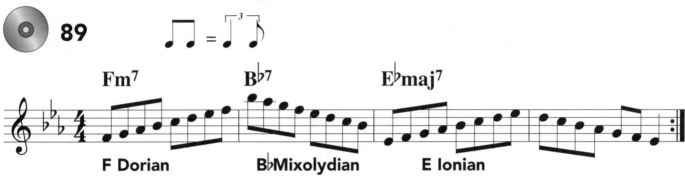

The next step is to improvise over the progression using the notes of the modes, as shown in the following examples.

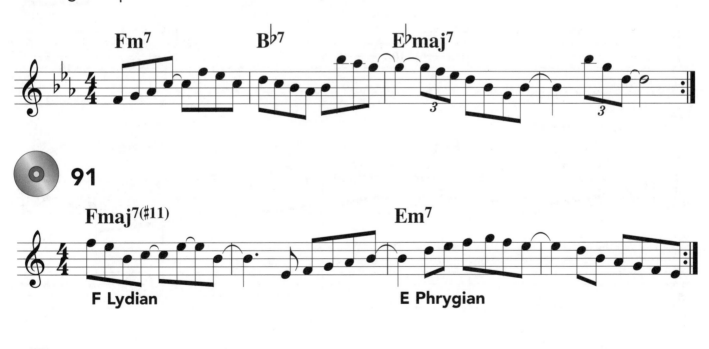

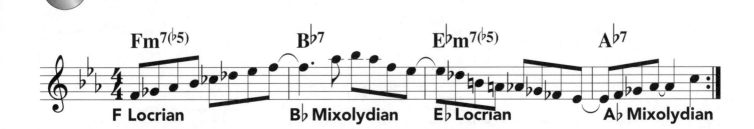

COMBINING MODES AND ARPEGGIOS

Here is a final solo which uses both modes and arpeggios. Analyze the notes against the chord changes and then make up your own phrases based on the ideas presented here. To improve your playing further, it is recommended that you now move on to *Progressive Jazz Lead Guitar Technique* which contains an in-depth look at Blues playing, along with minor keys, chord and scale substitution and many other important elements of modern Jazz playing. Keep practicing, keep listening to albums and above all, play with other musicians as often as possible.

 93   Many Things in One

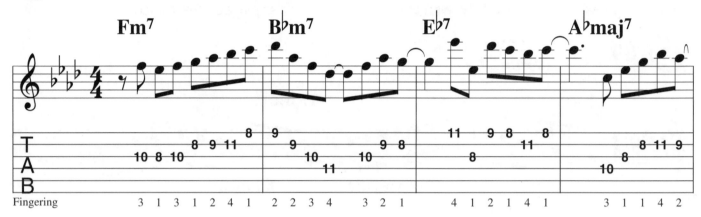

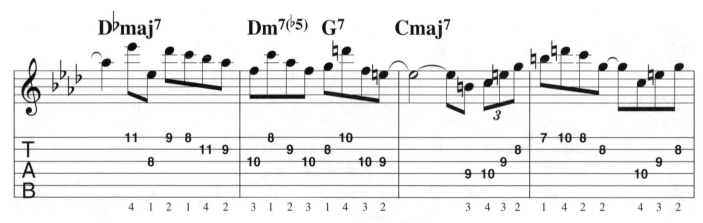

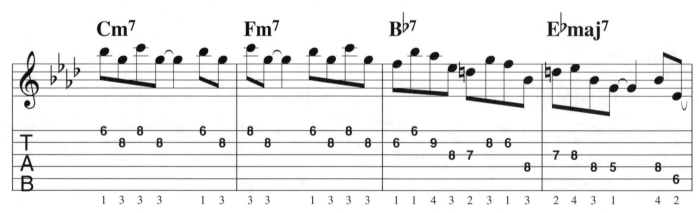

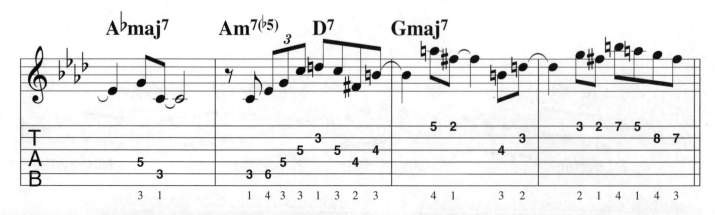

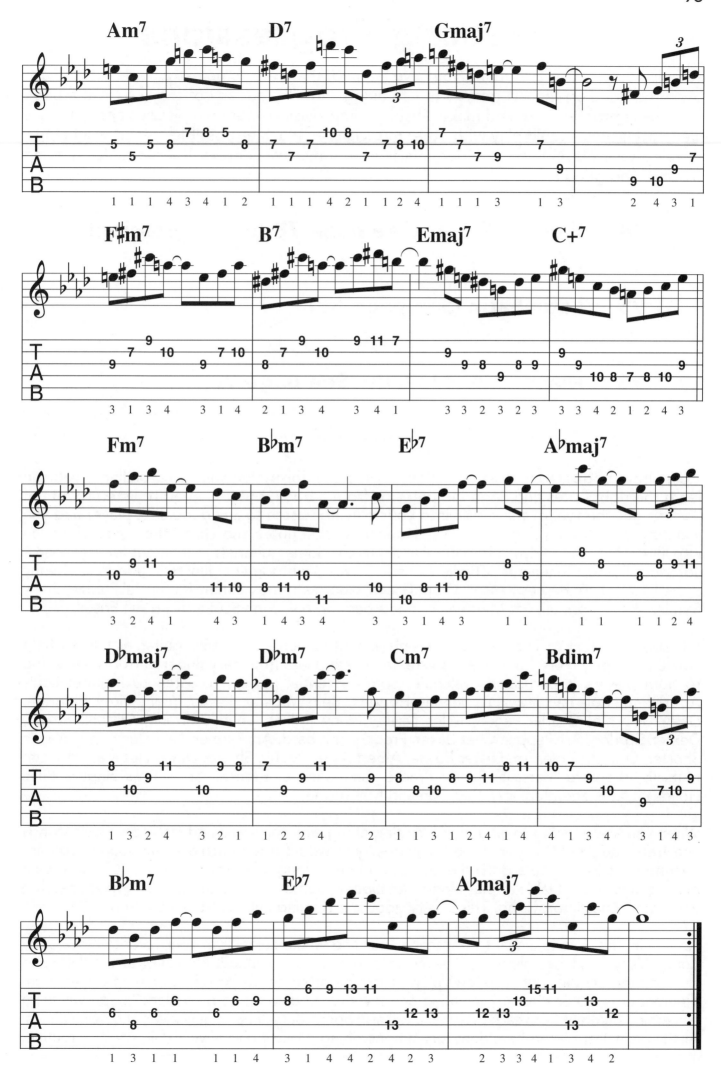

Jam Along Progressions

To help you practice everything you have learned, there are some extra tracks which have been recorded on the CD for you to jam along with. Try out any of the lines in the book with these progressions, and make a habit of improvising your own phrases and solos. As well as this, you should play with other musicians as much as possible, as this will help to develop your playing and also put your lines in a musical context. Keep practicing, keep playing, and good luck.

94   **Blues in B Flat (See page 78 for progression)**

95   **Latin Satin (See page 85)**

96   **Many Things in One (See page 92)**

Listening

Apart from books, your most important source of information will be recordings. You can learn the right notes and fingering patterns from a book, but you need to listen to lots of Jazz to get the feel of the music into your playing. Listen to any good Jazz player and you will hear intervals, arpeggios, modes, sequences, blue notes and chromatic notes all woven into lines which sound dynamic, natural and musical. Some guitarists to look out for are: Lonnie Johnson, Django Rinehardt, Charlie Christian, Wes Montgomery, Jim Hall, Joe Pass, Kenny Burrell, Herb Ellis, Barney Kessell, Grant Green, George Barnes, Jimmy Raney, Tal Farlow, Emily Remler, Bruce Forman, Pat Metheney, John Abercrombie, John Scofield and Bill Frisell.

It is also important to listen to musicians playing instruments other than guitar, as this will help you learn to play more from what you are hearing and less from easy finger patterns. Listening to horn players is particularly valuable. Some essential players to listen to include: Louis Armstrong, Coleman Hawkins, Johnny Hodges, Ben Webster, Lester Young, Roy Eldridge, Dizzy Gillespie, Charlie Parker, Miles Davis, Sonny Rollins, John Coltrane, Clifford Brown, Dexter Gordon, Art Pepper, Chet Baker, Freddie Hubbard, Art Farmer, Paul Desmond, Wayne Shorter, Ornette Coleman, Lester Bowie, Albert Ayler, Archie Shepp, David Liebman, Wynton Marsalis, Branford Marsalis, Randy Brecker and Michael Brecker, as well as singers Billie Holiday, Ella Fitzgerald, Sarah Vaughan and Mel Torme.

When you are listening to albums, try to sing along with the solos and visualize which strings and frets you would play and the techniques you would use to achieve the sounds you are hearing. This helps you absorb the music and before long, it starts to come out in your own playing. It is also valuable to play along with albums, sometimes imitating what you are hearing and other times improvising. This is very good ear training and is also a lot of fun.

As well as this, it is essential to transcribe lines and whole solos from your favorite players. By doing this, you will be able to analyse the lines to understand what it is you like about them and then incorporate them into your own playing. It is important to transcribe a variety of players from different eras rather than just imitating one favorite (who wants to be a clone?). You will learn something different from each player and will also open yourself up to new ideas and new sounds. All the great Jazz players have done lots of transcribing. Make it part of your daily practice routine.

PROGRESSIVE SCALES AND MODES FOR GUITAR
FOR BEGINNER TO ADVANCED

Progressive Scales and Modes gives the student a complete system for learning any scale, mode or chord and makes it easy to memorize any new new sound as well as building a solid visual and aural foundation of both the theory and the guitar fretboard. The book also shows you how to use each scale as well as how and why it fits with a particular chord or progression. The final section contains jam along progressions for every scale and mode presented in the book.

PROGRESSIVE GUITAR METHOD: THEORY
FOR BEGINNER TO ADVANCED

A comprehensive, introduction to music theory as it applies to the guitar. Covers reading traditional music, rhythm notation and tablature, along with learning the notes on the fretboard, how to construct chords and scales, transposition, musical terms and playing in all keys. A useful tool for songwriting and composition, and essential for any guitarist who wants to become a better musician.

PROGRESSIVE BLUES LEAD GUITAR TECHNIQUE
INTERMEDIATE TO ADVANCED

The central approach of this book is the development of musical technique, dealing with rhythm as it applies to lead guitar playing and concentrating on the development of phrasing and timing and how to really get the most out of the notes you play. Along the way, the book introduces the Blues scale and other important scales and arpeggios commonly used by Blues players. Also contains lots of great solos.

PROGRESSIVE BLUES GUITAR SOLOS
INTERMEDIATE TO ADVANCED

Contains a great selection of Blues solos in a variety of styles reflecting the whole history of the Blues tradition from early Delta Blues to contemporary Blues Rock. Demonstrates various methods of creating solos along with sections on vocal style phrasing, call and response, developing a theme, dynamics and the use of space. Many of the solos are written in the styles of Blues legends like Muddy Waters, John Lee Hooker, BB, Albert and Freddy King, Buddy Guy, Albert Collins, Peter Green, Magic Sam, Otis Rush, Eric Clapton and Stevie Ray Vaughan.

PROGRESSIVE ROCK GUITAR LICKS
FOR INTERMEDIATE TO ADVANCED

This book may be used by itself or as a useful supplement to *Progressive Rock Guitar Technique*. The licks throughout the book are examples of how the most popular lead guitar patterns can be used in all positions on the fretboard, and how various techniques can be applied to each pattern. Several Rock guitar solos are included to fully show how the licks and techniques studied throughout the book can be used to create a solo.

PROGRESSIVE JAZZ LEAD GUITAR TECHNIQUE
INTERMEDIATE TO ADVANCED
An in-depth study of the sounds used in Jazz lead guitar playing. Demonstrates how to make music from scales, modes and arpeggios, and enables you to easily understand what you are playing. Also contains systems for analyzing both rhythms and scale degrees as well as expressive techniques and various approaches to Blues playing. Contains lots of great lines and solos.

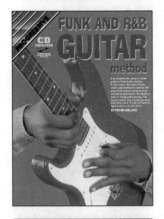

PROGRESSIVE FUNK AND R&B GUITAR METHOD
FOR BEGINNER TO ADVANCED
This book demonstrates many of the classic Funk sounds, using both rhythm and lead playing, since a good Funk player needs to be equally comfortable with both. A variety of chord forms are introduced within a framework that quickly allows the student to play confidently over the entire fretboard. Features an innovative approach to learning rhythms and applying them to riffs and grooves.

PROGRESSIVE FUNK AND R&B GUITAR TECHNIQUE
INTERMEDIATE TO ADVANCED
Covers a range of exciting chord sounds essential to Funk, along with the Dorian and Mixolydian modes and the use of harmonic intervals such as 6ths, 3rds, 4ths, octaves and tritones. Also features a thorough study of rhythms and right hand techniques such as percussive strumming and string muting. A range of Funk styles are examined, as well as some great Soul and R&B sounds.

PROGRESSIVE GUITAR METHOD: FINGERPICKING
BEGINNER TO INTERMEDIATE
Introduces right hand fingerpicking patterns that can be used as an accompaniment to any chord, chord progression or song. Also covers alternate thumb, arpeggio and constant bass style as used in Rock, Pop, Folk, Country, Blues Ragtime and Classical music. The book ends with several challenging and great sounding solos.

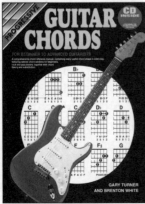

PROGRESSIVE GUITAR CHORDS
FOR BEGINNER TO ADVANCED GUITARISTS
Shows you every useful chord shape in every key. An open chord section for beginners contains the simplest and most widely used chord shapes in all keys. A bar chord section for the semi-advanced player who will need a thorough knowledge of bar chord shapes in all positions. A section for the advanced player listing the moveable shapes for chords widely used by Jazz guitarists. Other sections contain important music theory for the guitarist including scales, keys and chord construction.